May this supreme, peerless teaching,

The precious treasure of the Victorious Ones

Spread and extend throughout the world,

Like the sun shining in the sky.

GOLDEN ROSARY EDITIONS

*comprise oral teachings by
Khenchen Thrangu Rinpoche on the great
lineage masters of the Kagyu tradition.*

*They are reproduced through
the inspiration of H.H. Karmapa,
the blessing of Khenchen Thrangu Rinpoche,
and the guidance of Venerable Lama Karma Shedrup.*

*These editions are dedicated
to their long life and prosperity.*

Zhyisil Chokyi Ghatsal Trust
Publications

The Life
&
Spiritual Songs
of
Milarepa

by
Khabje Khenchen
Thrangu Rinpoche

ISBN Number: 1-877294-26-8

This publication is a joint venture between:

Namo Buddha Publications
P. O.Box 1083, Crestone,
CO 81131, USA
Email: cjohnson@ix.netcom.com
Thrangu Rinpoche's web site: www.rinpoche.com
and

Zhyisil Chokyi Ghatsal Trust Publications
PO Box 6259 Wellesley Street,
Auckland, New Zealand
Email: inquiries@greatliberation.org
www.greatliberation.org

Acknowledgments
We would like to thank Gabriele Hollmann for the enormous work of transcribing and editing this manuscript. We would also like to thank Jean Johnson for going over the manuscript. And, of course, we would like to thank Peter Roberts for carefully retranslating this manuscript and giving his advice on technical details. The songs on pages 53 - 55 are from *The Rain of Wisdom*, translated by the Nalanda Translation Committee under the direction of Chogyam Trungpa Rinpoche. © 1980 by Chogyam Trungpa. Reprinted by arrangement with Shambhala Publications Inc., Boston, www.shambhala.com

Notes
Technical words are italicized the first time that they appear to alert the reader that their definition can be found in the Glossary of Terms. The Tibetan words are given as they are pronounced, not spelled in Tibetan. We use B.C.E. (Before Current Era) for B.C. and C.E. (Current Era) for A.D.

Table of Contents

Ven. Lama Karma Shedrup Cho Gyi Senge Kartung

Foreword

The Golden Rosary Editions contain the spiritual biographies and teachings of the glorious Kagyupa lineage. The term "Golden Rosary" refers to this lineage of realized masters who have transmitted unbroken the profound Mahamudra teachings of the Lord Buddha to the present day. What makes these teachings so profound is that they contain instructions and practices which enable one to accomplish enlightenment in one lifetime.

One of the tremendous blessings of the Kagyu lineage is the diversity of lifestyles manifested by the lineage masters, showing that whatever our circumstances or lifestyle, we can practice these teachings and accomplish enlightenment. For example, Tilopa accomplished enlightenment while working as a menial labourer grounding sesame seeds. Others like Marpa were businessmen and had families. Marpa's student Milarepa was an ascetic who spent his life practicing in isolated caves, and one of his students, Gampopa, was a monk. Yet what they all had in common was that through practicing Mahamudra they all accomplished enlightenment. All this shows the great variety and power of the methods of Vajrayana for transforming one's mind through whatever circumstances. So similarly, if we practice Mahamudra with great diligence and effort we can achieve the fruition in one lifetime.

Therefore to read these spiritual biographies of the Kagyu lineage masters is a great inspiration to enter the path and they also provide encouragement and inspiration to continue when circumstances become difficult. In particular it is of great blessing to receive these teachings from Khenchen Thrangu Rinpoche, a master of great wisdom and compassion. Because he has directly realised Mahamudra and is a holder of this lineage he can transmit not only the words but the meaning.

So, I encourage all students to read these spiritual biographies and pray that it will inspire you to fulfil all the aspirations of the lineage masters. And may this merit cause the life and teachings of the great masters to flourish and remain for many eons benefiting limitless sentient beings.

Zhyisil Chokyi Ghatsal Trust
3/1 Franklin Rd, Ponsonby
Auckland, NZ

Biography of
Thrangu Rinpoche (b. 1933)

The lineage of the Thrangu Rinpoche incarnations began in the fifteenth century when the Seventh Karmapa, Chodrak Gyatso visited the region of Thrangu in Tibet. At this time His Holiness Karmapa established Thrangu Monastery and enthroned Sherap Gyaltsen as the first Thrangu Rinpoche, recognizing him as the re-established emanation of Shuwu Palgyi Senge, one of the twenty-five great siddha disciples of Guru Padmasambhava.

Khenchen Thrangu Rinpoche is the ninth incarnation of this lineage and was born in Kham, Tibet in 1933. When he was four, H.H. the Sixteenth Gyalwa Karmapa and Palpung Situ Rinpoche recognized him as the incarnation of Thrangu Tulku by prophesying the names of his parents and the place of his birth.

He entered Thrangu monastery and from the ages of seven to sixteen he studied reading, writing, grammar, poetry, and astrology, memorised ritual texts, and completed two preliminary retreats. At sixteen under the direction of Khenpo Lodro Rabsel he began the study of the three vehicles of Buddhism while staying in retreat.

At twenty-three he received full ordination from the Karmapa. When he was twenty-seven Rinpoche left Tibet for India at the time of the Communist invasion. He was called to Rumtek, Sikkim, where the Karmapa had his seat in exile. At thirty-five he took the geshe examination before 1500 monks at Buxador monastic refugee camp in Bengal India and was awarded the degree of Geshe Lharampa. On his return to Rumtek he was named Abbot of Rumtek monastery and the Nalanda Institute for Higher Buddhist studies at Rumtek. He has been the personal teacher of the four principal Karma Kagyu tulkus: Shamar Rinpoche, Situ Rinpoche, Jamgon Kongtrul Rinpoche and Gyaltsab Rinpoche.

Thrangu Rinpoche has travelled extensively throughout Europe, the Far East and the USA. He is the abbot of Gampo Abbey, Nova Scotia, and of Thrangu House, Oxford, in the UK. In 1984 he spent several months in Tibet where he ordained over 100 monks and nuns and visited several monasteries. He has also founded Thrangu Tashi Choling monastery in Boudhnath, a retreat centre and college at Namo Buddha east of the Katmandu Valley, and has established a school in Boudhnath for the general education of lay children and young monks. He also built Tara Abbey in Katmandu. In October of 1999 he consecrated the college at Sarnath which will accept students from the different traditions of Buddhism and will be open to Western students as well.

Thrangu Rinpoche, a recognised master of Mahamudra meditation has given teachings in over 25 countries. He is especially known for taking complex teachings and making them accessible to Western students.

More recently, because of his vast knowledge of the Dharma, he was appointed by His Holiness the Dalai Lama to be the personal tutor for the Seventeenth Karmapa Urgyen Trinley Dorje.

Preface

*T*wo thousand five hundred years* ago the Buddha gave a remarkable set of teachings in which he postulated that everyone experiences suffering. He further taught that to overcome this suffering, this feeling that the world is not going the way that we want it to go, could only be done by explaining the mind. The Buddha then spent the next forty years of his life giving teachings on how to overcome this suffering and how to attain complete freedom, that is complete liberation or awakening. The examination of mind involves first understanding why we suffer, then contemplating the causes of this suffering, and finally examining our mind through meditation. The meditation, which is common to all Buddhist traditions, is known as sitting meditation or Shamatha meditation in Sanskrit.

These teachings spread first throughout India and then gradually to most Asian countries. In the eleventh century the Moslems invaded India and destroyed most of these teachings in the country of their origin. However, a few centuries before brave pilgrims from China and Tibet had come to India risking life and limb and had collected these precious Buddhist teachings and taken them back to their own country and translated them into their language.

One such person was Marpa who came from Tibet and brought back a large numbers of texts of not only what the Buddha taught, but of Buddhist teachings which were practiced by the accomplished masters or siddhas of the eleventh century. The Buddhist practices of these siddhas were a living tradition passed down from guru to disciple with the disciple not receiving the teachings until the master had completely accomplished the practice and the pupil had shown that he or she was ready to receive them. In many ways one could say that these were the most important transmissions of the Buddhist teachings because they weren't simply words on a page.

Marpa received the complete Vajrayana practices of Hevajra, Chakramsamvara, and Vajrayogini. In addition, he received the six yogic practices of Naropa and the transmission for Mahamudra practice. By completely mastering these practices Marpa was able to achieve enlightenment in one lifetime.

Marpa brought back these teachings and transmitted them to Milarepa who is one of the greatest Buddhist saints to have ever lived. His incredible story of achieving enlightenment is told in *The Life of Milarepa* and is one of the truly inspirational books in Buddhism. This biography tells mainly the story of Milarepa's life. Milarepa's teachings on his practice of the Six Yogas and the Mahamudra meditation is mostly told in a second book called *The Hundred Thousand Songs of Milarepa* translated by Garma Chang.

Marpa received the teachings on a particular type of meditation called Mahamudra, which is a special meditation of the Vajrayana school of Buddhism. Mahamudra meditation does not involve the great accumulation of merit of the Hinayana, nor does it require the very scholarly analysis of emptiness of the Mahayana; rather it is the practice of looking directly into one's own mind and seeing its true nature.

For example, one day Tilopa asked Naropa to stretch a piece of cotton cloth across the ground and when he had done so, Tilopa lit the cloth and asked Naropa what he saw. Seeing the charred warp and woof of the cloth Naropa replied that he understood that the guru's instructions was like a fire which burned away the disciple's disturbing emotions which was like the cloth. This causes the belief in subtle reality to be destroyed and so the student cannot enter into a worldly living.

Thrangu Rinpoche is one of the most respected scholars of the Kagyu lineage of Tibetan Buddhism. He is recognized for not only having a tremendous scholarly background, but also for having great meditative insight into the Buddhist teachings. Every year since 1986 he has shared his wisdom and teachings with Western students through his *Namo Buddha Seminars* given at his monastery in Nepal. At the Namo Buddha Seminar in 1988 he gave a series of ten teachings on Milarepa's *100,000 Songs*. These *Songs* contain very detailed explanations of Buddhist dharma illustrating the yogi's spontaneous realizations. These songs of Milarepa can still be heard in the monasteries of Nepal and, one hopes, have not been forgotten by the people of Tibet.

Since these spiritual songs are often a distillation of a practitioner's lifetime of meditation, they sometimes need a commentary to explain all the nuances of what they mean. Due to the large number of *Songs* and the limited time of the Namo Buddha Seminar, Thrangu Rinpoche selected ten of the important *Songs* to illustrate important Buddhist teachings and gave extensive commentaries on them.

In *The 100,000 Songs of Milarepa* translated by Garma Chang the reader will find that the translation does not always correspond to the way in which the song is translated here. This is why we have included a translation of the parts of the *Songs* that are relevant rather than simply referring the reader to Chang's book.

Finally, the reader may feel that these stories of ghosts and demons and supernatural powers are simply folk legends from twelfth century Tibet. This certainly would be the orthodox Western historian's view. However, even today in the Far East there are great Tibetan practitioners who perform miracles similar to those described in The *100,000 Songs*. Many of the lamas and lay persons, including Western practitioners, have seen these "miracles" and so the Western reader is cautioned from simply dismissing the accounts of Milarepa as folk lore. The most important aspect of these stories is, of course, the dharma that shows us how to conduct our lives so that we may reach enlightenment for the benefit of all beings.

Clark Johnson, Ph. D.

The Life
&
Spiritual Songs
of
Milarepa

Marpa the Translator, Milarepa's root guru
1012 - 1097 C.E.

1

An Introduction to the Text

The Nature of the Buddhist Biography

*T*he text entitled *The Life of Milarepa*[1] could be termed a biography, but biographies in Buddhism are not quite the same as those by modern historians. A modern biographer looks for factual information, such as the exact date somebody was born and the historical dates of the various things they did. In Buddhism a spiritual biography or a hagiography is not concerned with the details of a person's life: whether Milarepa was born in this or that year makes no difference. What does it matter if he was born on the sixth instead of the seventh day of the month? Rather, Buddhist biographies are based on the essential elements of the individual's life: What motivation did they have? What practices did he do? How much diligence did they have? What results did they achieve? Finally, how were they able to help other beings? This kind of biography inspires faith, devotion, and diligence for spiritual practice and that is why spiritual practice is so very important.

Some recent Tibetan scholars have denounced the Tibetan tradition of biographies as uncritical, arguing that they contain only the good qualities of their subject and omit all the bad qualities. It is true that there are few details in these biographies; we are not told what kind of food Milarepa ate, or what kind of bed he slept on. These are not just historical accounts of someone's life. A spiritual biography is called *namtar* in Tibetan, which literally means "complete liberation." These biographies describe individuals who have rejected *samsara*, and through faith, devotion, diligence, and wisdom have attained complete liberation from the sufferings of samsara. These biographies therefore describe the process of *liberation* beginning with why the individual first choose to practice the *dharma*, how they met their teacher, what instructions were received, how that individual practiced them, and what results were achieved. These biographies have the purpose of inspiring the readers to become drawn to the dharma and be diligent in their practice.

The Characteristics of a Spiritual Biography

A spiritual biography can be said to have nine characteristics. These characteristics can be grouped into three sets, each containing two faults to be avoided and one good quality to be acquired.

The first set of three characteristics is comprised of being meaninglessness, being in error, and being meaningful. For example, it would be pointless to describe how tall Milarepa was; the information that he was five feet or four feet tall would be meaningless. The second characteristic of being in error would be something contrary to the facts, for example, to say that Milarepa was a very aggressive or lustful person. Obviously those two faults should be avoided in a namtar and rather the text should be meaningful. For example, the text should describe how Milarepa's experiences of suffering and impermanence caused him to turn to the dharma, meet his *guru*, and practice his guru's instructions correctly so that those reading the biography will understand how they themselves should also follow the dharma, practice the instructions, and accomplish the end result of *enlightenment.*

The next group of three characteristics is dedication to learning, debate, and practice. The first, dedication to learning, means that one feels one has to know and explain everything in detail, which is not that important. The second is dedication to debate. Dedication to debate means being engaged in the refutation of certain statements, answering objections to one's own views, and so on which is not of any importance. What is important for a text is the third characteristic of dedication to practice. One does not just hear and contemplate the teachings, or just debate it, but one actually gains control of one's own mind, eliminating faults, increasing positive qualities, and accomplishing benefit for oneself and for others.

The last group of three characteristics is deceit, propagation of violence, and eliminating suffering. The first, deceit, means the treatise is written in order to mislead people. The second is a propagation of violence. The advocating of violence occurs when texts engender an increase of cruelty and violence towards others, instead of compassion and altruism. Texts with those two characteristics should be avoided. The kind of text that should be studied is one that has the characteristic of providing a method to eliminate suffering.

Therefore a namtar should not have any of the characteristics of: (1) being meaningless, (2) being in error, (3) dedicated to study, (4) dedicated to debate, (5) one of deception, or (6) advocating the propagation of violence. Texts containing these characteristics should not be written; one that has been written should not be taught, and its teachings should not be practiced.

The kind of text that should be written, taught, and put into practice is one that has the three characteristics of being: (1) meaningful, (2) dedicated to practice, and (3) is a means to eliminate suffering.

The Hundred Thousand Songs of Milarepa

The biography of Milarepa (Tib. *mila namtar*) is clearly written and easily understood, as is its translation into English, so it does not require much additional explanation. However, there is also the collection of the spiritual songs of Milarepa entitled *The Hundred Thousand Songs of Milarepa* (Tib. *Mila Grubum*) and in this book I shall explain a selection of songs from ten of its chapters. *The Hundred Thousand Songs of Milarepa* were compiled by Tsang Nyön Heruka[2] an emanation of Milarepa, who also wrote *The Life of Milarepa*. Tsang Nyön was a *siddha* who had gained the appellation "Nyönpa" which means "crazy." He was one of three famous contemporary "crazy siddhas": Druk Nyön who was "the crazy man from Bhutan," U Nyön who was "the crazy man from U[3]" and Tsang Nyön who was "the crazy man from Tsang.[4]"

The life-story and songs of Milarepa inspire people to practice his lineage of instructions. This lineage consists of the path of means using the *Six Yogas of Naropa* and the path of liberation,[5] which is *Mahamudra* meditation.

In the *Karma Kagyu* transmission of his lineage, the ninth Karmapa taught the realization of Mahamudra in three texts. He explained Mahamudra in the long *The Ocean of Definitive Meaning*, the middle length in *The Mahamudra which Eliminates the Darkness of Ignorance*, and the short *Pointing Out the Dharmakaya*. These three texts provide us with a progressive path of meditation beginning with the *four ways of changing the mind*[6] and progressing to the stages of tranquillity or *Shamatha* meditation and insight or *Vipashyana* meditation[7] by explaining the methods of practice that lead to the ultimate experience.

A Prayer to Marpa, Milarepa, and Gampopa

First, I shall give a brief description of Milarepa, so that we may have faith in him. Milarepa was an exceptional master, because he had an exceptional guru, Marpa, and an exceptional pupil, Gampopa. Jamyang Khyentse Wangpo[8] concisely described these three masters in a short prayer that is regularly recited in the Karma Kagyu school. In this prayer one verse is dedicated to each of these masters with each verse describing three special qualities that the master possessed. The first four lines is a prayer to Marpa:

> Great courage took you to India many times.
> With great wisdom, you saw the true nature of all
>   phenomena.
> With great accomplishment, you performed miracles.
> I supplicate the great translator Marpa.

Marpa underwent considerable hardships to go to India three times. He did not do this for his own benefit, but he did this so that he could meet great gurus such as Naropa and Maitripa and receive the teachings from them and put them into practice. Not only did Marpa have the great confidence that he could receive these teachings, but he also had the confidence that he could introduce these teachings into Tibet and teach many pupils who would practice and embody them correctly and completely, and then transmit them on to their own pupils. He did this so that their lineages would grow and prosper throughout the future.

When Marpa went to India, met his gurus, and received their instructions, he didn't just learn these instructions but he also practiced the instructions and attained full realization. Through the power of his wisdom Marpa saw the true nature of all phenomena and attained the supreme accomplishment (enlightenment) within that very lifetime.

Marpa not only saw the true nature of phenomena, but as a sign of his attainment of the *dharmakaya* he was able to display a variety of miraculous powers to his pupils who were worthy, so as to engender faith, and have them follow the dharma.

The second verse is a prayer to Milarepa:

> With great power, you destroyed your enemies.
> With great hardship, you pleased your guru.
> With great diligence, you raised the victory banner
>   of practice.
> I supplicate the great yogi Milarepa.

Milarepa began by studying under a master of black magic and using his powers he destroyed and killed his uncles who had treated him, his mother and sister poorly. This, of course, created great negative karma that Milarepa would have carried into future lifetimes had he not regretted these actions and searched out a true *lama*, Marpa.

Marpa commanded Milarepa to build a succession of stone houses only to tell him to pull them down again. Despite the hardship involved, Milarepa's faith in Marpa never wavered, and he fulfilled Marpa's commands. This purified him of his negative karma, which pleased Marpa, his guru.

Milarepa, having received the instructions from Marpa, knew that the practice of these instructions was more important than any worldly activities. So Milarepa lived in various caves even if it meant that he had to go without food or clothes and practiced with diligence until he accomplished enlightenment. He then passed on his dharma teachings to many pupils thus raising the victory banner of practice.

The next verse is a prayer to Gampopa:

> The Great Vehicle awakened your heritage.
> Due to the Mahamudra your realization manifested
>   itself.
> Your great activity extended as far as space extends,
> I supplicate the great meditator Gampopa.

Milarepa had many disciples, but there were two main ones: Gampopa, who was said to be like the sun, and Rechungpa, who was said to be like the moon. Gampopa was an exceptional pupil who had been prophesied by Buddha Shakyamuni.[9] Gampopa was a physician who when he lost his family to a disease that he could not cure began seeking the dharma. He began by first studying under a *Kadampa* teacher and took ordination learning and practicing the *Mahayana* doctrine. Later when he heard some beggars discussing Milarepa he developed great faith in Milarepa, so he sought him out, became his student and received teachings from him.

Gampopa practiced the Mahamudra instructions he received from Milarepa and attained the ultimate result, the manifestation of the realization of Mahamudra, so that the special qualities of the Mahamudra experience and realization arose in his mind.

Gampopa accomplished the ultimate realization of Mahamudra and passed on the transmission of his teachings through four great pupils: Dusum Khyenpa (the first Karmapa), Tsultrim Nyingpo, Baram Dharma Wangchuk, and Pagmo Drupa, from whom the four primary and eight secondary Kagyu lineages subsequently formed.[10] These teachings on Mahamudra meditation and other *Vajrayana* practices have literally spread around the world, so the instructions of Marpa, Milarepa, and Gampopa have thus continued uninterrupted due to the extensive activity of Gampopa.

2

Six Songs of Longing for the Guru

*T*he Hundred Thousand Songs of Milarepa* are in three parts: the teachings Milarepa gave to non-human beings, the teachings he gave to his principal disciples, and the general teachings he gave to his ordinary pupils.

The first chapter of the book[11] begins with the section on teachings to non-human beings. It is entitled *Six Songs of Longing for the Guru*. These spiritual songs clearly teach the wish to abandon samsara, devotion to the guru, and meditation on compassion for non-human beings.

The story begins when Milarepa was practicing Mahamudra meditation in the Kyung dzong (Garuda-castle) cave in Chong lung (Carnelian-valley). One day he thought he would eat something but discovered that he had run out of food, water, and even firewood. He decided that he had been a little too diligent in his meditation in that he had ignored his physical welfare and that he should now pay a little attention to the material world.

There are some people who believe that they need to undergo the same hardships as Milarepa by being very poor and eating very sparsely. But in fact, deprivation is not necessary on the spiritual path. Hardship alone does not bring *Buddhahood*; it is through the practice of the dharma, of meditation, that one accomplishes Buddhahood. Milarepa had an overriding desire to meditate and thus underwent hardships because everything else meant little to him. Milarepa was so concentrated on meditation that he forgot all about food and clothing, and so ended up without any.

So, Milarepa left his cave to collect some firewood. A sudden gale began to blow his firewood away and when Milarepa held on to his wood he began to lose the cotton robe he was wearing to the wind. This put Milarepa into a dilemma of either holding onto his wood or to his robe, until he thought, "I've been meditating for so many years to overcome attachment to the self, but I haven't even been able to abandon my attachment to fire wood and this piece of cotton. If the wind wants to take my wood, then let it take it! If it wants my cotton robe then let it take it!" So he let the wind blow away both his firewood and his robe.

Milarepa was in such a state of physical exhaustion, due to his exertions and living on very little food, that he passed out. When he came to he saw his cotton robe was hanging from a tree. He took it down sat himself upon a stone and gazed into the east where he could see a white cloud far away. He thought, "Marpa is living in the land of Drowolung (Wheat-valley) just under that cloud. He also thought of his many dharma companions who would be there, receiving instructions and *empowerments* from Marpa. He then thought about this until he had an unendurable longing for that place, his guru, his fellow pupils, and his guru's teachings. With sadness, faith and devotion, he sang a spontaneous song, in which he said:

In the east there is a white cloud. Beneath that white cloud is Drowolung. In the hermitage in Drowolung, Marpa Lotsawa is living. In the past I was able to see him. If I could see him now, I would be so happy. I don't have enough devotion, but I long for my exceptional guru so intensely I would be so happy to be able to see him again.

The second verse describes Marpa's wife, Dagmema. She was very loving, particularly to Milarepa, so the verse says:

Dagmema showed more love to me than my own mother. If she were here and I could see her, I would be so happy. She is so far away and the journey to her would be difficult, but I long to see her.

Then he sang:

Now Marpa is in Drowolung and will be giving the four kinds of empowerments – the vase empowerment, the secret empowerment, the wisdom-knowledge empowerment and the word empowerment. If I could receive such profound empowerments now, that would make me so very happy. Though I am poor and have no offering for the empowerment, nevertheless, it is so fortunate to request and receive the four empowerments. I long for them and I long for my guru.

When one meets Marpa Lotsawa in the hermitage of Lho Drowolung, he gives the instructions which allows one to reach Buddhahood in one lifetime, within the one body: these are the instructions of the profound Six Yogas of Naropa. It is fortunate to dwell in Drowolung, to see Marpa Lotsawa and to receive the instructions of the profound Six Yogas of Naropa. If I could have that good fortune now, I would be happy. Although I don't have enough diligence to meditate on these instructions, they are profound, so that if I could receive them and meditate upon them, I would be happy.

There are many fortunate Dharma companions who are scholars and practitioners from U and Tsang who are staying at the hermitage of Drowolung. They receive empowerments and instructions together; when they practice the dharma together they compare their various experiences and realizations, examining them to see how good they are. When they receive instructions from the guru, the pupils compare their understanding of them, to see whether they have clearly understood their meaning or not. Due to this their experiences and realizations increase. If I could have that good fortune I would be happy.

I have faith and devotion in my guru, who is never apart from me, but my intense longing for him is unendurable; I am intensely miserable. So I am praying to you to dispel my sadness.

When Milarepa had finished singing this song the cloud in the east extended towards him. Upon its foremost tip was Marpa Lotsawa, more majestic than ever, mounted upon a white lion. Marpa said, "What is the meaning of this? Why are you calling me so loudly? Are you distressed that you can't receive the *blessings*[12] of the *three jewels*? Can't you meditate because you think too much? Are you pining for pleasures and worldly activities? What is it? Whatever is the matter, we are inseparable; I am always with you.

Therefore, practice the dharma well, preserve the teachings, and benefit other beings in the future." Milarepa was overjoyed to see Marpa, and sang a song, which says:

> I had sadness in my mind and so thinking of my guru's life: how he lives at Drowolung with his pupils and followers, teaching the dharma and bestowing empowerments. I felt great longing and devotion, and thus received the guru's compassion and blessing, terminating my nondharmic thoughts. I have disturbed my guru with my loud cries, but please forgive me and continue to look upon me with compassion.
>
> I am practicing with great diligence enduring the hardships of hunger, thirst, and cold. I offer this practice to my guru, in order to please him. I dwell alone in the mountains as a pleasing service to the *dakas* and *dakinis*. Though I disregard physical hardships, applying myself to the practice of the dharma as an act of service to the teachings of the Buddha. I will practice for as long as my life lasts, as a gift of dharma to the beings who are without a refuge, without a protector.
>
> If I'm going to die, I'll die; if I'm going to be sick, I'll be sick; but it will not make any difference to me. I shall practice considering it to be more important than anything else. This is my purification of negative karma and *obscurations*. Undergoing hardships is the necessary condition for developing experiences and realizations. Therefore, you, Marpa Lotsawa, have shown me great kindness in giving me the complete

empowerments and instructions that will enable me to accomplish Buddhahood through diligence. To repay that kindness I am practicing the dharma, so look upon me with compassion.

Having prayed in that way Milarepa's mind was filled with joy. He put his cotton robe back on, gathered up the firewood and returned to his cave.

When he entered his cave he saw that there were five strange Indian yogins, called *atasaras*,[13] in there. They had tiny black bodies and huge eyes. One of them was sitting on Milarepa's seat, teaching the dharma, another two were listening to him, another one was making food, and another was reading through Milarepa's texts. Then they all stopped what they were doing and stared at Milarepa who felt a little frightened. Then Milarepa thought, "I've been meditating in this place for so many years, but I've never offered any thanks by giving any *torma* offerings to the deity who is master of these lands, or to any of the local deities or spirits.[14] Therefore they have created this illusion. I must express my thanks for being in this place." So Milarepa sang this song:

This is a place of solitude, an excellent place for the accomplishment of Buddhahood. It is said that many *siddhas* have dwelt here in the past. This is an excellent place where I can live alone and practice that which is good. This is a pure place, with pure water, where the birds live free from fear without any care. The birds and monkeys are relaxed, free from worries and kind to each other. Such a place as this is very good for me and it is conducive to practice.

I dwell here meditating on the *bodhichitta* of aspiration and the bodhichitta of application.[15] It is perfect for me. Now that you have come, I will meditate on love and compassion towards you. Be happy and depart.

Milarepa finished his song, but the five yogins were very angry. They increased in number from five to seven and faced him as an angry group. Milarepa tried wrathful *mantras* against them, but they had no effect. Meditation on compassion and giving them teachings was no help either. Then Milarepa thought, "I am Marpa Lotsawa's pupil. He gave me the realization that all phenomena are nothing other than the mind. Therefore these beings are nothing but the creations of my own mind and I shouldn't be afraid of them." Milarepa then sang a song about his confidence expressed through analogies.[16]

The nine-story stone tower built by Milarepa as instructed by his teacher
Marpa (see page 6). It was built on the edge of Marpa's land. In the
1930s this tower stood alone, but since that time a small monastery
seen surrounding the tower has been built.

3

Songs of the Snow

he third chapter of the collected songs of Milarepa is
Songs of the Snow.[17] This chapter describes Milarepa's
practice of meditation, especially his practice of *tummo*
and the sign of heat that he generated as a result of this practice.

It must be pointed out that the main point of Milarepa's life
story is not that we can only accomplish the dharma by practicing
in the way that he did. It is an example of the diligence that leads
one to the ultimate goal. It would be good if we could develop a
diligence like Milarepa's, but even if we can't, a development of
dharma practice over a long time can still attain the same result.

The first chapter describes how Milarepa subdued demons in
Tramar Chonglung. The second chapter describes how Milarepa
went to Lachi snow-mountain and subdued the leaders of many
demons there. From this he became famous as a lama with great
powers who could subdue demons.[18]

Then Milarepa went to stay at Nyanang and other places near
to Lachi mountain. He said, "Staying in the middle of villages is
depressing. I must go on my own to a place of solitude where I
can accomplish my practice and my guru's instructions. Living in
a village is not a very good thing anyway, so I shall go to stay on
Lachi mountain for a second time."

Milarepa's pupils made a request, saying, "Great lord, your only concern is the welfare of beings, therefore give us teachings. If you remain here with us for the winter it will be of very great benefit. You must please stay here. Winter on Lachi mountain is very difficult with so much snow and cold." Milarepa replied, "I am a pupil in the lineage of Naropa, so I am not afraid of such things. Marpa Lotsawa commanded me to avoid distractions and to practice in solitude."

As Milarepa had decided to leave some of his pupils requested to escort him to the mountain. All Milarepa took with him was a little *tsampa*, rice, meat and butter. He was escorted to Lachi mountain where he took up his residence in Dundul Pumoche (The great cave of the subjugation of Mara) cave. His escort started their return journey to the village but the weather turned bad. It snowed heavily and they reached the village with great difficulty. It snowed continuously for nine days and nine nights[19] so that the route between the village and where Milarepa was staying became cut off for six months. Milarepa's pupils were certain that he must have died and that there was no way he could have survived, so they made funeral offerings to him in the fourth Tibetan month (about May to June). They decided that they should at least go and collect his body so that they will be able to make offerings to it. Therefore, some of them forced their way through the snows to reach Lachi mountain.

When they neared Milarepa's cave they saw a snow leopard upon a rock and thought, "Milarepa's body will have been eaten by that snow leopard and we are not even going to be able to bring back his body." When they reached the spot where the snow leopard had been they saw human footprints. They wondered, "What is this? Is it some deity or spirit?" When they came close to Milarepa's cave they heard him singing and then calling out, "Hurry up! Where have you been that you're so late getting here?" When they got to the cave they discovered that Milarepa had already prepared a meal for them.

The pupils then asked, "How did you know we were coming?" Milarepa replied, "I saw you when I was sitting on that big rock over there." But they said, "But all we saw was a snow leopard on that rock, so what do you mean?" Milarepa then said, "That was an emanation of myself. I have meditated for so long that I have mastery over my mind and *subtle winds*,[20] so I can manifest many emanations."

Milarepa was in good health but he hadn't had enough food to keep him alive, so they asked him how he had survived. Milarepa said, "I don't need much food because of my practice of meditation and sometimes dakinis bring me a portion of their *ganachakras*. Therefore I only need to eat a spoonful of tsampa to keep myself alive. But also, in the fourth month, I had a vision of you surrounding me and offering me a great deal of food, after that I didn't need to eat at all." They said that was the time when they had made the funeral offerings to him, thinking he was dead. Milarepa said, "This proves that when people do good actions for the sake of someone who has died, it really does help them."

Then the pupils requested him to return to the village. At first Milarepa refused, saying, "My meditation is going well here, so I'm not going to leave." The pupils insisted, saying, "People will accuse us of leaving you here to die and they will be very angry with us, so you must come back this one time to the village with us." Milarepa agreed to come and so they set off together with some going on ahead to tell the villagers that Milarepa was alive and on his way. A great number of villagers came to welcome him and escort him to the village. When they asked Milarepa's how he was, he replied with a song:

I am happy that today we have met here and all are still alive. This old man has many songs, so I am singing in answer to your question. Listen well.

Saddened by samsara, I did not stay in the village, but went to Lachi snow-mountain. It was as if the sky and the earth had planned a snowstorm. So many clouds gathered and the sun and moon could not be seen, the stars and planets could not be seen, it was as if they had been thrown into prison. The snow fell for nine days and nine nights with snowflakes coming down as large as birds and snowflakes as small as sesame seeds. I was in a high place and the dark mountains around me were all turned white.

When this great snow fell, all people's homes were changed into prisons because they could not leave. Animals, deprived of food, suffered a famine. The wild animals also had no food. Neither did the birds in the sky. Mice hid under the ground like a treasure and animals of prey had nothing to eat.

The blizzard that fell upon me, the winter wind and my thin cotton robe competed with each other to see who could make the winter coldest for me. As I am one of a lineage of heroes, I didn't run away and all ended well. Therefore I believe that in the future the teachings of the Practice Lineage will spread, there will be many siddhas, and I, Milarepa, will be famous for my accomplishment of the dharma. You my pupils will have faith in me and the future will be good and the Buddha's teachings will spread. That's how I am. How are you?

The villagers danced with joy. Milarepa's experience and realization intensified and he danced too, leaving his footprints and imprints from his staff all over the rock beneath him.

When he arrived in Nyanang village, his pupils said, "You are in good health and must have developed exceptional realizations and experiences in your meditation. Please tell us about them." In reply Milarepa sang a spiritual song about his experiences and realizations in which he describes his view, meditation, conduct and commitment:

My view is the realization of the true nature of the mind exactly as it is; the mind is seen to be unborn, empty. There is nothing to be viewed. There is the destruction and disappearance of the viewed and the viewer. I have obtained such an excellent view.

My meditation is an unbroken continuity of clarity, like the constant flow of a river. This is meditation on the true nature of the mind. The true nature of the mind never changes; the meditation is unceasing, with no difference between periods of meditation and periods of non-meditation. It is as if one has lost the capacity to distinguish between meditation and meditator. Everything is meditation, so that meditation has great diligence.

My conduct is that there is no change in the mind's fundamental clarity, in whatever I do. The interdependence of phenomena is empty. All distinction between acts that are done, and the individual who acts, are destroyed.

My commitment is free of hypocrisy, artifice, hope, and worry. The distinction between a commitment that is kept and the keeper of a commitment is ended and destroyed. I have this excellent commitment.

The result of this is that the mind is seen as the dharmakaya. There is a spontaneous achievement of benefit for myself and others. There is no distinction between a result that is achieved and one who achieves. I have this excellent result.

This is an old man's song about the happy time he has had. In my retreat I was cut off by the snow. I was looked after by dakinis. I had the best of drinks – the water of melted snow.

Milarepa's pupil, Shakya Guna, expressed his joy that Milarepa had returned without harm, that none of his pupils had died, and that they have all met again. He requested Milarepa to give them a dharma teaching on the six months that he had spent in retreat. Milarepa replied with a song on the signs of accomplishment from his six months of practice:

Saddened by worldly activities I went to Lachi mountain, where I stayed in the solitude of the Dundul Pukpa cave, practicing for six months, here I experienced the six signs of accomplishment.

The six external objects are:
If it obstructs, it is not space. If they are countable, they are not stars. If it moves, it is not a mountain. If it diminishes or increases, it is not the sea. If it can be crossed by a bridge, it is not a great river. If it can be grasped by the hand, it is not a rainbow.

Six inner faults are:
Looking up at the planets is not the view. This means that the view should be free of conceptualization and identification.

Meditation on the view should be free of stupor or the agitation of thoughts, otherwise, it is not a valid meditation.

When we arise from meditation and engage in conduct, that conduct should be free from the distinction of good conduct to be adopted and bad conduct to be rejected.

One who has the true view, meditation, and conduct is a yogin. A yogin should always be free from thoughts, otherwise he or she is not a true yogin. That yogin must have wisdom that does not fluctuate between clarity and obscuration. If it does, that is not true wisdom.

The ultimate result is freedom from suffering, birth, and death. If there is birth and death, then the result is not Buddhahood.

The six kinds of bondage that bind one to non-liberation from samsara are:
Anger causes one to fall into and remain in the hell realms. Anger is a bondage that binds one to hell. Miserliness is a bondage that binds one to the realm of the *hungry ghosts*. Stupidity is a bondage that binds one to the world of animals. Desire is a bondage that binds one to the world of humans. Envy is a bondage that binds one to the realm of the *jealous gods*. Pride is a bondage that binds one to the realm of the *gods*.

These six *kleshas*[21] are bondages that bind one to non-liberation from the *six realms* of existence.

There are six aspects to the path that leads to liberation from these bonds, from samsara:
If there is great faith, one will be able to enter the valid path, therefore faith is the path to liberation.

If with great faith one follows a guru who is learned and self-controlled, one will go along the path to liberation.

If while following the guru one keeps one's commitments to the guru, this is the path to liberation.

If one has faith, relies on a guru, and keeps unbroken commitments, and then one wanders in the mountains, one will be able to truly accomplish the path to liberation.

If wandering through the mountains one stays alone avoiding distractions, one will be able to practice the dharma properly, and therefore this is the path to liberation.

If remaining in solitude one practices, that is the path to liberation.

There are six profundities:
The innate natural profundity is the mind at rest in an uncontrived state. This natural state is not newly created, but is primordially innate within us.

When there is no distinction between internal and external, and everything is pervaded by the mind, and by knowledge, this is called the profundity of knowledge.

When the all-pervading knowledge is free from fluctuation in its clarity, and is ever-present, it is called the profundity of wisdom.

When that wisdom pervades everything, this great pervasion is the profundity of the true nature of phenomena.

When that expanse of the true nature of phenomena is free of loss and change, when it is always present, that is called the profundity of the *essential drops* (Skt. *bindu.)*

When that state is free of loss or change and is continuous, that is the profundity of experience, the experience of meditation.

These are the six profundities possessed by the confident.

There are the six kinds of bliss that are the results of the path of means such as tummo:
When the heat of the tummo practice blazes in the body, there is bliss.

When the karmic winds that move through the left channel (the *lalana*) and the right channel (the *rasana*), and enter the central channel (the *avadhuti)* are transformed into wisdom-air, there is bliss.

When the flow of bodhichitta descends in the upper body, there is bliss.

When the lower body is pervaded by the bindu, there is bliss.

When the white and red elements come together in the middle of the body, there is bliss.

When the body is permeated by immaculate bliss,
there is bliss.
These are the six kinds of ultimate bliss in yoga.

4

The Rock Sinmo
in the Lingpa Cave

*M*arpa had told Milarepa that he should meditate on Palbar mountain. Milarepa went there and discovered the Lingpa Cave to be very pleasant, and so he meditated in that cave.[22] One day he heard a loud voice coming from a crack in the rock. Milarepa got up and looked but decided it was just a meditator's illusion and sat down again. Then a bright light shone out from the rock. Inside the light there was a red man astride a musk-deer that was being led by a woman. The man gave Milarepa a slight blow and then disappeared in a gust of air. The woman changed into a red female dog that seized Milarepa by the big toe of his left foot and would not let go. Milarepa, understanding that this was a manifestation of a Rock Sinmo[23] sang her a song.

> Rahula, who is the deity of the eclipse, please do not be an enemy to the sun and moon that shine their light from the sky down onto beings.
>
> Snow blizzards, please do not attempt to harm the white lion when he is wandering on the snow-mountains.

Concealed pit filled with pointed stakes, do not harm the tigress who dwells within the jungles, who is the champion amongst the beasts of prey.

Hooks, do not harm the golden fish that swim in lake Mapam.

Hunter, do not harm the vulture in the sky that seeks for food without killing anything.

I am Milarepa, practicing for my benefit, and the benefit of others. I have forsaken this life's wealth and possessions, food, and clothes. I have developed the bodhichitta and I am attaining Buddhahood within one lifetime. Therefore, Rock Sinmo, do not harm me.

The Rock Sinmo still wouldn't release Milarepa's foot and replied to Milarepa with a song delivered by a disembodied voice using practically the same poetic images, and concluding with:

You say that you accomplish the welfare of yourself and others, that you have developed the bodhichitta, and that you are achieving Buddhahood within one lifetime so that you will become a guide for all the beings in the six realms of existence.

However, when you meditate one-pointedly, strong tendencies from your previous lives cause illusions to appear. The tendencies are causes, the illusions are conditions, and the result is that your own thoughts appear to you as enemies, as demons. If your own thoughts did not appear as your own enemies, I, the Rock Sinmo, could not appear to you.

The demons and spirits appear due to negative tendencies, and come from the mind.
If you do not know the nature of your own mind, even though you tell me to leave, I won't.

Milarepa thought that what the Rock Sinmo had sung was very true. He replied to her with a song using eight images:

Your words are very true. Nothing could be more true. I have wandered through many places but have never heard anything as beautiful as your song. Even if I questioned many scholars, I would never hear a higher meaning. The eloquent words from your mouth are like a golden needle that pressed onto the heart dispels the heart-air[24] and dispels the darkness of delusion and ignorance, causing the lotus of the mind to blossom, causing the torch of self-knowledge to blaze, and causing wisdom to awaken.

When I look up into the sky, I think of *emptiness* that is the true nature of phenomena. Therefore I have no need to be afraid of material phenomena.

When I look at the sun and moon, I think of the fundamental clarity of the mind. Therefore stupor and agitation cannot harm me.

When I look at a mountain's peak, I think of the stability of meditation. Therefore loss or change in meditation cannot harm me.

When I look at a river, I think of the unbroken continuity of meditation experience. Even if a sudden condition appears, it can cause no harm.

When I look at a rainbow, I think of the unity of appearance and emptiness, in which emptiness does not harm appearance, and appearance does not harm emptiness. As I have realized the union of appearance and emptiness I am not afraid of *eternalism* and *nihilism*.

When I look at the reflection of the moon on water, I think of ungraspability, so that thoughts of grasped and grasper cannot harm me.

When I look inwards at my own mind, I think of a naturally radiant butter-lamp in a bowl. Therefore the dullness of ignorance cannot harm me.

Because I listened to your instructions my meditation and self-knowing wisdom has become clear. I am free of obstacles from demons and obstructing spirits. You have given many teachings, and clearly understand the nature of the mind, so why have you become a demon? You have become a demon because you harmed beings and ignoring the law of karma. Therefore you should now contemplate karma and the harmfulness of samsara, and abandon all evil actions. I was only pretending to be afraid of demons. I was playing a trick on you. Don't think that it was real.

The Rock Sinmo now had faith in Milarepa, and stopped trying to harm him. She answered him with a song in which she says:

I am fortunate to have met Milarepa. It has been good to hear the Dharma being taught. I am what I am because I harmed many people.

Milarepa, deciding that she must be bound to an oath, replied to her with a song in which he said:

These elevated words you speak will be of no use to you. You are in this body because you have harmed others. You must abandon those negative actions, practice what is good, and be of assistance to yogins.

What you need now is to pay careful attention to cause and effect, and you must promise to support all dharma practitioners, and be a friend to all yogis in particular.

The Rock Sinmo, now that she had true faith in Milarepa, manifested her body to him and sang a song in which she said:

I have committed many negative actions, I had strong defilements and extreme malevolence and intolerance. I am fortunate to have met you and to have received the dharma from you. I repent creating an illusion and attacking you. I vow that I shall no longer harm others and that I will be a friend to yogins practicing dharma in retreat.

Milarepa then taught her the dharma and in particular he sang a song in which he said:

There is a demon that is greater than you – attachment to the self. There is a demon that is more evil than you – evil intent. There is a demon that is wilder than you – thoughts.

Take an oath to subdue them and enter the dharma. If you do not break your word all will be well with you.

When Milarepa had completed his song, the Rock Sinmo took that vow and disappeared. At dawn the Rock Sinmo, with her entourage of beautiful males and females wearing beautiful jewellery, appeared to Milarepa, bringing him many offerings. The Rock Sinmo said, "I have a spirit's body because I harmed beings in a previous life. I request that you to teach me the dharma" singing the following song:

I have met many siddhas, but you are the one who had the greatest kindness and blessing for me. I request the dharma from you. Some give the teachings containing the *provisional meaning* and some give the *Hinayana* teachings, but these are unable to subjugate the mind's defilements. Others speak many words and give many teachings, but cannot provide refuge from suffering and the conditions for suffering. You are a *nirmanakaya* of the Buddha, and therefore you have realized the true nature of phenomena. Please bestow upon us the profound teachings that come from your own mind.

In reply, Milarepa sang her a song with twenty-seven images (three for each of nine verses) in which he said:

I don't usually sing on the *ultimate truth*, but as you have asked me to, I shall.

(1) Thunder, lightning, and clouds appear from the sky and merge back into the sky.

(2) Rainbow, mists, and fog appear from the air and merge back into the air.

(3) Honey, fruit, and crops arise from the earth and merge back into the earth.

(4) Forests, flowers, and leaves arise from the hillside and merge back into the hillside.

(5) Rivers, foam, and waves arise from the ocean and merge back into the ocean.

(6) Latencies, clinging, and attachment arise from the ground consciousness and merge back into the ground consciousness.

The mind has latencies[25] that have been laid down throughout beginningless time. These latencies result in our perceptions. The mind also clings to the perceptions of things that we desire. Finally, there is an attachment to phenomena which mind takes as being truly real. These latencies originate and arise from the *ground consciousness.*

The seventh consciousness is the *afflicted consciousness,* which is a continuous attachment to the self whether we consciously think of it or not. Whether these seven consciousnesses are present or not, the continuity of the mind never ceases. There is always a non-apparent consciousness, that is, the ground consciousness from which all the latencies of appearances originate. Therefore, latencies, clinging, and attachment arise from the ground consciousness, and when they disappear, they then merge back into the ground consciousness.[26] Milarepa continues:

(7) Self-knowledge, self-clarity and self-liberation arise from the mind and merge back into the mind.

When meditating on the true nature of mind, the mind knows itself, it has natural clarity, and it naturally liberates itself from the kleshas. These three qualities of the self-awareness of mind, the natural clarity or luminosity of mind, and the natural liberation of mind are not newly created from meditation, but arise from the nature of the mind itself and then merge back into the nature of the mind.

(8) Non-arising, non-cessation and indescribability arise from the true nature of phenomena (Skt. *dharmata*) and merge back into it.

First there is non-arising, at the end there is non-cessation, and in-between these there is indescribability. These are the characteristics of the true nature of phenomena.

(9) The appearance of demons, the belief, and the concept of demons, arise from yoga and merge back into yoga.

The appearances, belief, and concepts of demons may arise on the *conventional level* or relative level and from the practice of yoga they merge back into it. Obstacles and obstructing spirits are just manifestations of the mind. If one doesn't realize that they are empty,[27] one will believe them to be demons. If one does realize that they are empty, there is a natural liberation from demons.

There are many delusions that occur in samsara: outer delusions, inner delusions, defilement delusions, and so on. The mind is the source of all these delusions.[28] All delusions naturally cease when there is the realization of the nature of the mind. The true nature of the mind is a natural fundamental clarity that is empty, beyond coming or going. Though we perceive numerous external phenomena, they are all delusions manifested by the mind. They are empty by nature, but nevertheless appear. Though they appear, their nature is empty. This is the inseparability of emptiness and appearance.

Even meditation is just a thought, even non-meditation is just a thought. Whether one meditates or not, the nature of the mind does not change. Therefore, even a belief in meditation and non-meditation is a cause of delusion.

Phenomena have no reality, they are like space. Their emptiness must be understood. If you wish to have the correct view, you must see the emptiness that transcends the intellect. If you wish to have correct meditation, you must meditate without distraction. If you wish to have correct conduct, it must be effortless and natural. If you wish to gain the full result, hope and fear must be abandoned.

This is my teaching to you.

This ends the teaching of Milarepa on the absolute or ultimate view.

Chogyal Namkhai Norbu demonstrating the yogic posture of Milarepa.

5

Songs on Yolmo Snow-Mountain

I have chosen this chapter[29] from the collected songs of Milarepa because Yolmo mountain is very near to Kathmandu, and there are persons here (in Kathmandu where the seminar is being given) who feel a strong connection with Yolmo.

Marpa had told Milarepa what places he should practice in. One of these was Yolmo snow-mountain, and so Milarepa came to Yolmo and stayed in a cave called Tapuk Senge Dzong (Tiger cave at Lion castle) in the forest of Singaling (The Land of Lions). While he was there local deities caused him no obstacles; they manifested themselves in peaceful forms and took an oath to serve and honor him. Milarepa's meditation progressed well.

One day five young men and women came to see him and asked him to teach them the dharma. They said, "This is such a terrifying place, the quality of someone's practice would be bound to be very unstable. Has this happened to you?" In answer to their question, Milarepa sang them a spiritual song in which he said:

Yolmo has pastures, flowers, trees, forests, monkeys,
birds, bees, in summer and winter, autumn and spring.

Here I meditate on emptiness. Sometimes many thoughts arise, and these aid my meditation. This is very good.

I do not accumulate bad karma, and therefore I have good health. I will have thoughts that will disturb my body and make me uncomfortable. Nevertheless, that is beneficial for my meditation experience and so this is very good. I am therefore free from the defilements and free from birth and death, and this is good.

Though deities and spirits are malevolent and create illusions, it only increases my realization. This is very good.

I am free from sickness, but if suffering occurs, it appears as bliss, which is very good.

I have the pleasure of different kinds of meditation experiences, but sometimes when I jump, run or dance, I am even more blissful.

The five pupils felt great faith on hearing Milarepa's song. He then gave them instructions, which they then meditated on and attained good qualities, which pleased Milarepa. He sang them a song about the kind of conduct they should have, in which he said:

There are many Dharma practitioners, but you are very fortunate to meditate upon this path. You are practicing to attain Buddhahood within one lifetime using one body. Therefore do not have attachment to this life. Many good and bad actions are done for the sake of this life, and this prevents you from properly following the path of the dharma.

In serving the guru, you should not feel proud that you have done so well, as this prevents the accomplishment of the goal.

In keeping your commitments, you should not associate with ordinary people, which brings the danger of your breaking your commitments.

When you are studying you should not feel proud that you have understood the meaning of the words, as this will cause the disturbing emotions to blaze up like fire and ruin your good activities.

When you meditate with your companions in the dharma, you should not have many tasks to perform, as they will cause distraction and be an obstacle to the dharma.

After those general instructions, Milarepa gave specific instructions on how his students were to conduct themselves on the path of means involving such profound practices as the Six Yogas of Naropa by giving them the profound instructions of the *oral transmission*:

In doing these meditations, you should not use the powers developed from the oral transmission for the subjugation of demons or for the giving of blessings. If you do, your own being will become demonic, many obstacles will occur, and you will fall into worldly activities.

When practicing the dharma there will sometimes be meditation *experiences and realizations* of the true nature of your own mind. When these occur, do not brag that you are doing well and do not display clairvoyant powers. If you talk about signs of progress that you have attained, you will develop pride, envy, anger, and the signs will diminish. You need to understand and abandon all these faults.

Then Milarepa's students asked him how they could practice self-sufficiency, and Milarepa sang some general instructions saying that they must practice well, have firm faith and devotion, and so on. They did practice well, and with great faith in Milarepa they offered him a *mandala* of gold and asked for an instruction on the essence of view, meditation, and conduct. Milarepa said that their practice was better than an offering of gold, and returned the gold to them. Then he sang a song in which he said:

The view, meditation, conduct and result are the foundation of the *mantrayana*.

The view of the mantrayana is how we should understand the true nature of phenomena. Intellectual knowledge of the view, however, is not sufficient to reach enlightenment because we have to meditate on what we have to understand.

Just engaging in meditation is also not sufficient to gain enlightenment because we have to know if our meditation is correct or not. Finally, to reach enlightenment we have to engage in pure conduct when we are not meditating.

The essence of the mantrayana is engaging in the correct view, proper meditation, and pure conduct. Each of these has three objects.

The Buddha's view has two aspects: the *sutra* and mantra views. In the sutra path we engage in understanding the true nature of phenomena by primarily engaging in logical arguments. In the mantra path, however, we engage in the understanding of the nature of phenomena through direct perception of mind.

There are three aspects to this mantrayana view:

(1) All appearances and existences are subsumed within the mind. All external forms, sounds, tastes, smells, and tactile sensation arise within the mind. The mind's sensations of happiness, suffering, defilements, thoughts, and anything else are also derived from the mind itself.

(2) What is mind? It is clarity and knowledge. It is not a material thing. It can think and change, it can engage with lucidity in all kinds of thoughts.

(3) However, the mind itself cannot be identified, as its nature is emptiness. While some teachers first introduce their pupils to emptiness and then to clarity, Milarepa introduces the clarity of the mind first and then introduces emptiness by pointing out that this clarity cannot be identified.

These are the three aspects of the mantrayana view of the true nature of the mind.

The three aspects of meditation are:

(1) Many thoughts appear in meditation. If the nature of mind is not identified, the thoughts become a problem; they become solid and an obstacle. However, when the true nature of the mind is realized, although thoughts arise, they are liberated as the dharmakaya.

(2) When thoughts are naturally realized to be the dharmakaya, the clear knowledge of the mind is a state of bliss that is free from suffering. Meditation is then accompanied by the experience of bliss.

41

(3) This meditation is not the creation of something new. Delusion has been dispelled by the mind resting in its own natural state, without alteration or artifice. The mind must rest, be relaxed in the nature of the mind itself.

The three aspects of conduct are:

(1) In the mantrayana one does not need to deliberately accomplish the ten good actions. The practice of good actions will occur spontaneously from the realization that comes from meditation.

(2) Similarly, the ten unvirtuous actions will be spontaneously avoided without any need to deliberately control one's actions. With the realization of the nature of mind one does not need to have contrived conduct.

(3) There will also be no need to deliberately contrive remedial actions, to engender realization through effort. If one rests relaxed in the natural state of the mind, the realization of clarity and emptiness will naturally arise.

Finally, the three aspects of result are:

(1) According to the Buddha's exceptional view of the mantrayana, *nirvana* and Buddhahood are not located in some other place so we have to go someplace to get them. They are also not newly created or achieved.

(2) Samsara is not like garbage that has to be thrown away. There isn't anything that can be thrown away. The very nature of samsara is nirvana, whether we realize it or not.

(3) Nirvana is not something to be created and samsara is not something to be eliminated because our mind is Buddhahood. There is no Buddhahood that is other than us; it is the nature of our own mind.

When we have gained the elimination of all the negative qualities and gained all the positive qualities of realization, it is the unchanged nature of our own mind, exactly as it is, which is Buddhahood. While we do not realize this, we are under the power of the defilements and wander in samsara. When we realize the true nature of the mind, there is the conviction that the mind is Buddhahood.

In this way view, meditation, conduct, and result have three aspects each, making twelve aspects in all, or as Milarepa says, the twelve nails hammered into them. There is an additional nail that is hammered in, a thirteenth nail, which applies equally to view, meditation, conduct, and result and that is the nature of phenomena, which is ungraspable. It is an emptiness that transcends all extremes, all conceptualization.

Who is it that hammers in these thirteen nails? It is the guru who introduces the pupil to recognition of the ungraspable nature.[30] If we analyze too much, the mind becomes confused and the nails will not go in. However, when we understand the innate nature exactly, the nails will be hammered in. These thirteen nails are the wealth that belongs to all dharma practitioners. Milarepa says, "They have arisen in my mind. Take pleasure in them and practice them."

Then Milarepa sang them another song:

> You must have diligence and faith when you practice.
> You must practice in solitude. Yolmo mountain is an
> excellent place to practice.
>
> Having followed my own advice in my own
> practice of meditation, I enjoy the most perfect
> happiness.

6

The Story of
Nyama Paldarbum

*T*he fourteenth chapter[31] of *The Hundred Thousand Songs of Milarepa* contains the teachings that Milarepa gave in response to the questions of Nyama Paldarbum. She asked Milarepa many questions and the answers Milarepa gave her are profound and beneficial to our own practice.

One autumn Milarepa came to a place named Gepa Lesum, where the people were bringing in the harvest. He was asking the people for food and a young girl named Nyama Paldarbum said, "Go to that house over there and I will come to you soon and give you food."

Milarepa went to the door of the house and tapped on it with his staff. There was no response. He tapped again and an old woman came out who said, "You so-called yogins do a lot of begging and when there's no one at home you go in and steal, which is exactly what you were planning to do!"

Milarepa then sang her a song describing the suffering of old age and how in the midst of those sufferings we must practice the dharma and follow a guru. When he had finished the old woman was filled with regret and felt faith in Milarepa. With her hands together she supplicated him with tears streaming from her eyes.

Paldarbum arrived at this point and thought that the yogi must have hit her. "What do you think you're doing, hitting an old lady?" she asked him.

The old lady said, "He didn't hit or insult me, I insulted him. Then he gave me dharma teachings that have aroused great faith in the dharma in me. I'm crying because I feel great regret for what I said to him. I'm very old now, but you're still young, so you should serve this lama, Milarepa, and request the dharma from him."

Paldarbum said, "You are both amazing. If you are Milarepa, then I am very fortunate to meet you. I have heard that when pupils listen to the account of your lineage they develop great faith and their perceptions are transformed. I have heard that you have very profound instructions. What are they?"

Milarepa could see that this girl had the karma to be an excellent pupil and so he sang her a spiritual song that described the profundity of his lineage. The usual description of his lineage is the succession of gurus – Tilopa, Naropa, Marpa – however, here he describes his lineage as the dharma which begins with the Buddha.[32] Therefore the source of the Vajrayana teachings is described to be the three kayas.[33]

Milarepa sang:

The dharmakaya is the all-pervading wisdom of the Buddha's mind, the all-pervading Samantabhadra, who is not an individual Buddha but represents the compassion and wisdom of Buddhahood.

The dharmakaya gives rise to the *sambhogakaya,* which is beautified by the eighty major and minor signs physical signs.

The sambhogakaya is a manifestation of form for pupils. This is called Vajradhara, which is not to be confused with the dharmakaya Vajradhara. This Vajradhara is not an individual Buddha but represents the changeless continuity of the sambhogakaya.

> The nirmanakaya that benefits beings is the Shakyamuni Buddha who has manifested to guide impure beings.
> I am a yogin who possesses the lineage that is exceptionally superior because it originates from the three kayas.

Paldarbum said, "This is an excellent lineage, but one needs a *root guru* from whom one can directly receive the instructions. What kind of root guru did you have?" Milarepa could have answered quite simply that his guru was Marpa Lotsawa, but he sang her a song of the outer, inner, and ultimate gurus:

> The outer guru is the one who communicates the continuity of knowledge through signs. He or she is the guru who teaches the instructions through symbols and other various methods.
> The inner guru is the one who teaches the continuity of wisdom and causes the direct recognition of the true nature of the mind.
> The ultimate guru is the one who teaches the ultimate truth by increasing the clarity of our wisdom until the final result is attained.
> I am a yogin who possesses the lineage of these three gurus.

Paldarbum then asked, "One needs to receive an empowerment from a good guru. What kind of empowerments have you received?" Milarepa could have answered, "I have received the empowerments of *Hevajra* and *Chakrasamvara*, but instead he sang a song in which he said:

> I have received the outer, inner and ultimate empowerment.
> The outer empowerment is the vase being placed upon the crown of the head and is the symbolic use of ritual objects.
> The inner empowerment is the demonstration that one's own body is the body of the deity. It is the meditation that one's body is the body of the deity, so that one receives the blessing and the subtle channels (Skt. *nadi*) and subtle drops (Skt. *bindu*) of the body are empowered.
> The ultimate empowerment is that which causes the direct recognition of the nature of the mind.
> I am a yogin who has received these three empowerments.

Paldarbum said, "Those are very good empowerments. But having received these empowerments, one needs instructions so that one can follow the path. What kind of instructions did you receive?" Milarepa replied with a song:

> I have received the outer, inner and ultimate instructions.

The outer instructions are to listen, contemplate, and meditate in order to gradually understand the meaning.

The inner instructions are to be resolute, have intense diligence in meditation that will be the basis for the accomplishment of the final result.

The ultimate instructions are to have the continuous presence of realization and experience, which comes from diligence in meditation.

I am the yogin who has these three instructions.

Paldarbum said, "You have received good instructions. But when one has received instructions, one needs to go into the mountains to practice the dharma. What kind of dharma practice have you done?"

In reply Milarepa sang of the outer, inner and ultimate Gocara practice,[34] which are forms of the "cutting practice in which one cuts through one's attachment to the self:

The external chö is to wander in fearful places where there are deities and demons.

The internal chö is to offer one's own body as food to the deities and demons.

The ultimate chö is to realize the true nature of the mind and cut through the fine strand of hair of subtle ignorance.

I am the yogin who has these three kinds of chö practice.

Paldarbum said, "That is a very good chö practice. When yogins do this practice, they recite "pai"[35] in order to transform bad circumstances into the path. What is the meaning of this phat? To this Milarepa replied with a song about the outer, inner and ultimate phat:

> The outer phat is the dispelling of the thoughts that prevent a stable meditation and it is also the gathering in of these thoughts.
> The inner phat is clearing away the dullness or agitation that affects the mind's awareness in meditation.
> The ultimate phat is resting in the true nature of the mind.
> I am the yogin who has these three kinds of phat.

Paldarbum said, "This phat is very good. When you practice in this way what kind of mental states occur?" Milarepa sang of the mental states of the uncontrived ground, path, and result:

> The uncontrived ground is resting in the all-pervading true nature, the true nature that pervades all phenomena.
> The uncontrived path is not a gradual progress, but a direct arrival.[36]
> The uncontrived result is the true nature as Mahamudra.
> I am a yogin who has those three mental states.

Paldarbum said, "This is marvelous, it's like the sun shining upon me. What kind of confidence have you gained from your practice?" Milarepa sang of the confidences of view, meditation, and result:

The confidence in the view is the realization of emptiness. This is the view that there are no deities nor any demons so that one cannot obtain benefit from deities or receive any harm from demons.

The confidence in meditation is the absence of an object of meditation. This means that there can be no distraction.

The confidence in the result is the absence of hope to achieve it. This means there is the absence of fear of failure.

I am a yogin who has these three confidences.

Paldarbum felt great faith in Milarepa. She prostrated to him, invited him in, served and honored him, and said, "I am definitely going to practice the dharma, so please keep me in your compassion." Then she sang a song to Milarepa describing her many faults with the basic meaning of the song being, "I will sincerely practice the dharma. Please give me a practice that is simple to understand and easy to do." Milarepa, pleased with her, replied with a song:

Although you truly wish to practice the dharma, it is not enough to give up worldly activities. You must follow my example and practice without distraction.

Paldarbum then described in a song what her normal life is like:

In the day there is never-ending work. In the night I am fast asleep. Morning and evening I am a slave to food and clothes. I have never had the chance to practice the dharma.

Milarepa then sang to her a song on the four aspects of renunciation necessary for true dharma practice:

The next life is far away from this life. Have you prepared for this journey with food and clothes? The way to prepare for that journey is to practice generosity.

In order to receive food, clothes, and wealth in future lives you should give them in this lifetime. There is, however, an obstacle that prevents this generosity to future lives, miserliness. Miserliness or hoarding may seem beneficial in this lifetime in that one accrues food and clothes and other possessions, but in the long run it harms you because miserliness causes poverty in the next lifetime. Therefore you must recognize that miserliness is an enemy and cast it away behind you.

The next lifetime is darker than this lifetime. Therefore you must prepare a torch to illuminate that darkness. This is done by meditation on the fundamental clarity of the mind. Ignorance is the obstacle and the enemy of clarity. Ignorance may seem pleasant and beneficial superficially, but it is actually harmful and you must recognize it as an enemy and cast it away behind you.

The next lifetime is more frightening than this lifetime, so you must find a guard that will protect you. This guard is the practice of the dharma. Relatives dissuading you from dharma practice are the enemy. They may be helping and loving towards you, but ultimately they are harming you. Therefore you must recognize these relatives to be an obstacle and cast them away behind you.

The next lifetime is a longer, more desolate road than this lifetime, so you will need a horse so that you can travel along it easily. That horse is diligence. The enemy of diligence is laziness that will deceive you into thinking it is beneficial, although ultimately it is harmful. Recognize laziness to be an enemy and cast it away behind you.

When Milarepa had sung this song, Paldarbum felt great faith in Milarepa. He told her, "You don't have to change your name or cut off your hair.[37] A person can have hair and also accomplish Buddhahood." Then Milarepa taught her how to practice through a song of four analogies and five meanings:

O young lady, Paldarbum, listen wealthy lady, endowed with faith. Look up into the sky, and practice meditation free from fringe and centre. Look up at the sun and moon, and practice meditation free from bright and dim. Look over at the mountains, and practice meditation free from departing and changing. Look down at the lake, and practice meditation free from waves. Look here at your mind, and practice meditation free from discursive thought.

Then Milarepa instructed her in the physical and mental practices and sent her to meditate. When she returned some time later she sang of her experiences and doubts:

> O Jetsun Rinpoche, O supreme yogin, I am able to meditate on the sky; but when clouds arise, how should I meditate? I am able to meditate on the sun and moon; but when heavenly bodies move, how should I meditate? I am able to meditate on the mountains; but when trees and shrubbery blossom, how should I meditate? I am able to meditate on the lake; but when waves arise, how should I meditate? I am able to meditate on the mind; but when discursive thoughts occur, how should I meditate?

This means that she can look at the mind, nevertheless she is disturbed by the thoughts arising within it. Milarepa sang her a song to further her understanding and clear her doubts:

> O young lady, Palderbum, listen wealthy lady, endowed with faith. If you are able to meditate on the sky, clouds are manifestations of the sky. Once more resolve this manifestation; once more resolve your mind.
>
> If you are able to meditate on the sun and moon, the stars and planets are manifestations of the sun and moon. Once more resolve this manifestation; once more resolve your mind.
>
> If you are able to meditate on the mountains, the trees and shrubbery are manifestations of the

mountain. Once more resolve this manifestation; once more resolve your mind.

If you are able to meditate on the lake, the waves are manifestations of the lake. Once more resolve this manifestation; once more resolve your mind.

If you are able to meditate on your mind, discursive thoughts are manifestations of your mind. Once more examine the root of discursive thought; once more resolve your mind.

What this means is that if you see your own mind, then what you see is that the mind's essence or nature is emptiness. When you see that, you also see that the nature of whatever thought arises in the mind is also emptiness. When this is experienced directly, then these thoughts dissolve in their own place, which means right there or right here. Thoughts are not driven out or sent somewhere else; they do not go away, they simply dissolve naturally because they are seen.

7

The Encounter with Naro
Bönchung at Mount Kailash

Many Westerners now go to see Mount Kailash. It is a place where Milarepa practiced and performed miracles, leaving his handprints on the rocks and so on.[38] Therefore I shall go through the twenty-second chapter of *The Hundred Thousand Songs of Milarepa*[39] that describes Milarepa's experience there.

In the *Abhidharma* it is said that north of Bodhgaya, beyond nine dark mountain ranges and a snow mountain range there is the mountain Gandhamadana and the lake Anavatapta.[40] Milarepa believed Mt Kailash to be Gandhamadana, and the nearby Lake Mansarovar to be Anavatapta. On the other hand, the Sakya Pandita believed that Kailash and Mansarovar were not Gandhamadana and Anavatapta. However, the eighth Karmapa, Mikyo Dorje, and many other Kagyu masters have stated this mountain and lake is Gandhamadana and Anavatapta.

Marpa had told Milarepa that if he practiced at Lachi and Kailash mountain he would gain exceptional experiences and realizations, and would develop the great qualities that will benefit his pupils. So, to fulfil his guru's instructions, Milarepa went to Mount Kailash. The local deities of Kailash and Mansarovar greeted him on his arrival, prostrating to him and making offerings to him. They offered the mountain and the lake as places of practice to Milarepa and all his pupils. The deities also promised to help them when they practiced there by increasing the conditions that were conducive to their practice.

Naro Bönchung was in residence there at this time. He was an excellent practitioner of the Bön tradition[41] and had thereby attained some miraculous powers and clairvoyance. He had heard that Milarepa possessed inconceivable miraculous powers and clairvoyance, so he came to welcome Milarepa and his pupils as they arrived at the shore of Mansarovar.

Though he knew who Milarepa was, he pretended he didn't and asked, "Where have you come from and where are you going?" Milarepa answered, "We are going to Mount Kailash to practice meditation."

Naro Bönchung then asked, "And who are you?" and Milarepa answered, "I am Milarepa." Naro Bönchung then said, "Kailash and Mansarovar are very famous, but when you actually see them they're not anything special. You're the same, very famous, but nothing special in person. But even if Kailash and Mansarovar and you are really wonderful, this area is under the control of my tradition. It is our land and our mountain. So those who stay here have to follow the Bön tradition.

Milarepa said, "This mountain and lake belongs to the Buddhist tradition because the Buddha foretold of their existence. In particular my guru Marpa told me that I must practice meditation here. I am not just following my own wishes. That you live here is very good. It will be better if you continue to live here and follow the Buddhist tradition. If you're not going to practice Buddhism it will be best that you go somewhere else."

The reason Milarepa and Naro Bönchung argued in this way was not due to sectarianism, but because it is best that people keep to their own particular tradition; that way they will gain the final goal. But if they mix different traditions, their practice will not progress.

The Bönpo said, "If it's true that you have great miraculous powers, we should have a miracle contest. Whoever wins will be the master of Mt. Kailash. Now I shall perform a miracle." Naro Bönchung then straddled the lake with his left foot on the near shore and his right foot on the opposite shore. Standing thus he sang a song in which he said:

> Mount Kailash is very famous, but when you see it, it's just a snow covered mountain-peak. There's nothing wonderful about it.
>
> Lake Mansarovar is very famous, but it's just a depression filled by river water. There's nothing else there.
>
> Milarepa is very famous, but he's just a naked old man lying on the ground and singing. There's nothing wonderful about him.
>
> We Bönpos have an exceptionally superior teaching. There is the Bön Kaya, and the Bön deity who is the great King of wrathful deities, who has nine heads and eighteen arms and many emanations. His sister is Sipay Gyalmo ("Queen of Existence").
>
> The Bön dharma is superior. As a sign of that superiority, I manifest this miracle.

Milarepa then did a miracle. Without his body growing larger or Lake Mansarovar becoming smaller, he covered it entirely with his body and then he sang a song in which he said:

> Buddha Shakyamuni sits upon a lion throne on Gridhrakuta[42] mountain. The Buddha's teachings are exceptionally superior. His body, inseparable from his wisdom, is the dharmakaya Vajradhara. The one who rests in the meditation united with that dharmakaya, is Tilopa, the nirmanakaya. His pupil is the great *pandita* Naropa, and Naropa's pupil is Marpa Lotsawa.
>
> The blessing has been transmitted from Vajradhara through Tilopa, Naropa and Marpa to me. I have gained superior realizations and experiences.
>
> I am the famous Milarepa. In accordance with Marpa's command, I have come to meditate at Kailash. Meditating here I will accomplish complete benefit for myself and for others. Mount Kailash is very famous. The snow covered peak is a symbol of the purity of the Buddha's teachings. Mansarovar lake is very famous, being filled with water is a symbol of the cessation of phenomena into a state of equanimity.
>
> I am the famous Milarepa. An old man lying naked is a symbol of the abandonment of the concepts of perceiver and perceived. I sing because all appearances appear to me as books, as teachings. Then I give these teachings in the form of songs. That is why Milarepa is famous.
>
> In my realization and experience, outer appearances and the internal mind are inseparable. Thus, by gaining power over the mind I have gained

power over external appearances and can accomplish miracles.

I have no need of miracles such as yours that depend upon the help of a deity. As my miracles are superior to yours, Mount Kailash belongs to me. If you practice the Buddha's dharma that will be beneficial to all. If not, as you are defeated by my miracles you must go and live somewhere else.

Then Milarepa performed another miracle. He lifted up the entire Mansarovar lake upon his fingertip, without causing any harm to the creatures that lived in its waters.

Naro Bönchung said, "This time your miracle is a little better than mine, but I was here first, therefore we should consider this a draw. You say that I should leave if I refuse to practice Buddhism, but I will never abandon the Bön tradition. Therefore I will perform another miracle and if you can do a better one I will leave this place and go and live somewhere else."

Then Naro Bönchung proceeded to circumambulate Mount Kailash counter-clockwise,[43] while Milarepa circumambulated clockwise, until they eventually met each other.

Naro Bönchung seized Milarepa's hand and said, "You must circumambulate counter-clockwise." Milarepa answered, "No you must go clockwise," and they pulled each other in opposite directions leaving their footprints on stone as they did so. Due to the superiority of Milarepa's powers Naro Bönchung was made to go round the mountain clockwise.

When they had nearly finished going around, Naro Bönchung said, "Now this next time we should go counter-clockwise," but Milarepa said, "Well, that depends entirely on how strong you are. If you pull me along I'll have to go." So Naro Bönchung replied, "Well, we can find out which one of us is the strongest by seeing who can carry the biggest stone."

Naro Bönchung carried a large stone to where they were, but Milarepa brought a bigger one and placed it on top. Naro Bönchung said, "You've defeated me twice, but twice is not conclusive. We must compete once more." Milarepa answered, "There is no real contest between us, it's just like a game for me. I am bound to win, but so that future generations of practitioners can see the superiority of the dharma I'll do a another miracle."

Naro Bönchung went to the eastern side of Kailash and Milarepa went to the western side. Milarepa extended his leg through and under the mountain and made a footprint in Naro Bönchung's retreat. Milarepa said, "Now you do the same thing back," but Naro Bönchung couldn't.

Naro Bönchung insisted that they should have another contest, as a few miracles didn't prove anything. Again they circumambulated in opposite directions until they met. It then began to rain heavily so Milarepa said, "We should build ourselves a shelter."

Milarepa gathered rocks by simply pointing at them, and then told Naro Bönchung to bring some, but he failed to bring any by miraculous powers. Milarepa, just by staring at rocks, placed one on the right, one on the left, one at the rear and one on top as a roof. He then decided it was too high so he climbed on top and pressed it down with his foot, leaving a footprint on the stone.

After he had come down, he decided it was now too low, so he went inside and pushed it up with his hand leaving a handprint on the ceiling. In this way he created what is now called Zutrul Puk[44] or "The Miraculous Cave" which can be seen today.

After this miracle Naro Bönchung conceded. Milarepa then sang a lengthy song explaining how these miracles could be done. He does this by explaining it in terms of view, conduct, and result:

The Buddhist view is free from extremes and transcends the intellect. The belief that things are real is the source of thoughts and defilements. There is also the view that things do not exist. That is also a delusion. One might think that if there is nothing that exists, that there must be nothing. But if the existence of things has no reality, then their non-existence has no reality either.

The true nature of phenomena transcends existence and non-existence, and also neither existence or non-existence. The view that transcends these extremes also transcends the intellect, because it is not a view gained by thoughts that conceive the identity of something, but it is gained by the wisdom of meditation. This view is beyond the scope of the ordinary mind and therefore is a source of power to accomplish miracles.

There are two reasons why meditation is the source of miraculous power: non-distraction and objectlessness. Meditation is habituation to a state free of distraction. If meditation has an object on which the mind thinks, there will be attachment and that will give rise to the defilements that create the sufferings of samsara. Therefore I rest in a state of meditation that has no object, in which I directly see the true nature. That meditation is a source of power to achieve miracles.

Conduct can also yield the power of miracles and clairvoyance. I have a conduct that is free of the effort to reject or cultivate the various thoughts that arise in the mind. I rest relaxed in the true nature, which results in an uncontrived, relaxed, spontaneous manifestation of power to accomplish perfect miracles.

The result, the "self-liberation," also brings powers which when it is attained, causes the continuity of compassion, wisdom and power to not cease. There is a variety of qualities that are free from worldly attachment that are self-liberating.

This power of the result is derived from the direct recognition of one's own true nature. It is not a new creation, the developing of it is not going to some other place. Ignorance and delusion are due to not realizing the true nature as it is. The direct recognition of one's own true nature brings freedom from extremes and conceptual elaborations, and this leads to miraculous powers.

The purity of commitments (Skt. *samaya*) in which there has been no transgression also brings the power to achieve miracles. This is due to fulfilling the guru's instructions on meditation, diligence and particular practices, and it is due to the commitments to be free of any stain.

Practice is a source of the power to perform miracles, because all appearances are made to aid the development of realizations and experiences. If circumstances conducive to meditation occur, they can then facilitate diligence in meditation without the presence of pride. When deleterious circumstances and obstacles occur, they don't overpower or depress the practitioner, but are themselves made the basis for meditation. Therefore difficult circumstances are preferable in terms of the development of powerful meditation that has the power to perform miracles.

I, the yogin Milarepa, have the power to do miracles. This is due to my diligence, dedication, and endurance. When there are difficulties I do not feel afraid. My diligence does not last for just a month or year, but continues until the final goal is attained.

Due to my miraculous powers the Buddha's teachings will prosper at Mount Kailash. This has occurred due to the kindness of the Buddhas.

8

Invitation from the King of Kathmandu of Mön

*T*n chapter twenty-seven of *The Hundred Thousand Songs of Milarepa*,[45] Milarepa was staying in solitude in a cave on Katya mountain in the Nyishang Gurta,[46] in the area of Mön.[47] While there he was keeping silence and resting in a continuous stream of meditation.

During that time some hunters came along and saw Milarepa, motionless and staring. They thought he was a demon, and ran away, but then summoning up their courage, they returned ready to shoot him with their poisoned arrows. They asked him, "Are you a human being or a demon?" but Milarepa did not respond at all. They fired their arrows at him but they could not pierce his body. They decided to throw him over a cliff, but they couldn't lift his body. They stacked wood around him and set it on fire, but Milarepa didn't burn. They carried him to a wide river and threw him in, but Milarepa, rose up out of the water, perfectly dry, still in the *vajra posture,* and floated back up to his cave and back onto his meditation seat.

The astounded hunters left the mountain and told the nearby inhabitants about this amazing yogin that was living there. Milarepa's pupil Chirarepa, who had only recently become his pupil when he was a hunter who had come across Milarepa on the mountain, said, "That must be my Tibetan lama that you are talking about. He is a true siddha. He even taught the dharma to my dog and the deer when I was hunting, making them sit together and meditate."[48]

The reputation of Milarepa spread throughout Nepal. The King of Patan[49] and Bhaktapur[50] developed great faith and devotion towards Milarepa. The King dreamt that *Tara* told him, "You have Benares cotton and a yellow myrobalan[51] fruit. There is a great Tibetan yogin presently staying at the Katya cave. If you offer these things to him it will be of great benefit to you."

The king sent a man who could speak Tibetan to find Milarepa. When he came to Milarepa's cave and saw how he had forsaken material life and was remaining in meditation all the time, he felt great faith and was certain that he had found Milarepa. Nevertheless, in order to avoid any mistake he asked, "What is your name? Isn't it terrible to live like this, without anything to eat or drink? Why have you given up all possessions?"

Milarepa replied, "I am Milarepa, the yogin from Tibet. There is a great purpose to not having possessions." He then explained what he meant in a song:

> I have no desire for wealth or possessions, and so I have nothing. I do not experience the initial suffering of having to accumulate possessions, the intermediate suffering of having to protect and keep possessions, nor the final suffering of losing these possessions. This is a wonderful thing.
>
> I have no desire for friends or relations. I do not experience the initial suffering of forming a mental attachment, the intermediate suffering of

having a disagreement, nor the final suffering of parting from them. Therefore it is good to be without friends and relations.

I have no desire for pleasant conversation. I do not experience the initial suffering of seeking conversation, the intermediate suffering of wondering whether it will continue, nor the final suffering of the conversation deteriorating. Therefore I do not delight in pleasant conversation.

I have no desire for a homeland and have no fixed residence. I do not experience the initial suffering of partiality of thinking that "this is my land and that place isn't." I do not experience the intermediate suffering of yearning for my land. And I do not experience the final suffering of having to protect my land. Therefore it is better to have no fixed abode.

When Milarepa had sung this song, the man felt great faith in him and returned to the king and gave a detailed account of his meeting with Milarepa. The king said, "You must go back and invite Milarepa to come here. If he refuses, offer him this Benares cotton and yellow myrobolan from me.

The king's emissary returned to Milarepa and said to him, "A Dharma king is reigning in Kathmandu and Patan. He has sent me to invite you there. You must come there."

Milarepa replied, "I don't go into towns, and I don't know anyone who lives there. I certainly don't know any kings. I don't like fine food or drinks and I don't like having any possessions. I don't know any stories about dharma practitioners who die of hunger or cold. A lama who stays with a king will become lost. In obedience to Marpa Lotsawa's commands, I travel from place to place, practicing. It is best if you return to your king."

The emissary said, "He is a very great king. You're just an ordinary lama, so he has only sent one man on foot to invite you. It would be better if you came back with me." Milarepa replied, "No, that's not how it is. I'm not an ordinary person, I am a great king, a world-emperor, a *Chakravartin*. There is no one who is my equal, no one who is as powerful as me."

The king's man said, "If you're a world-emperor, you must have the seven royal possessions of a chakravartin. So where are they? No, you're just an ordinary person. If you're a wealthy king you'll have to prove it to me." In reply Milarepa sang a song that taught the seven aspects of enlightenment as the seven royal possessions of a chakravartin:

> Your king and ministers yearn for happiness, but with a kingdom like mine, this life and all future lives are filled with bliss.
>
> The first of the seven royal possessions is the precious wheel that can take the king anywhere swiftly and easily. I possess the precious wheel of faith. It takes me from samsara to nirvana. With faith and devotion I can enter any virtuous activity easily, so that I am swiftly taken to nirvana.
>
> The second royal possession is the precious wish-fulfilling jewel that spontaneously fulfils one's own wishes and the wishes of others. My second royal possession is wisdom, the wisdom of ultimate and relative truth, which brings the attainment of the state of Buddhahood. By knowing the individual capabilities and aspirations of beings, I turn the wheel

of dharma[52] for them fulfilling the hopes of all – the Hinayana vehicle for the lower pupils, the *pratyekabuddha* state for those of medium capability, and the Mahayana for those with superior capability.

The third royal possession is the precious queen who is very beautiful and adorned by a variety of jewellery. My third royal possession is good conduct – the dharma practitioner who maintains correct conduct is beautiful, because he or she is free of the stains of faults. Correct conduct develops all good qualities, like being adorned by jewellery.

The fourth royal possession is the precious minister who maintains and improves the kingdom's wealth. I have the royal possession of meditation through which I gather the accumulations of merit and wisdom.

The fifth royal possession is the precious elephant that can carry the great burden of the emperor's wealth. I have my conscience, so that if someone benefits me I know that I must not ignore them, but repay their kindness. All beings have shown me kindness and so I must help them all. If I give them the Buddha's teachings they will eventually reach Buddhahood. Therefore I take upon myself the burden, the responsibility, of giving the Buddha's teachings to all beings.

The sixth royal possession is the precious horse, the emperor's mount, which takes him easily to any land he wishes to go. I have the royal possession of diligence, which takes me from self-attachment and defilements to selflessness.

The seventh royal possession is the precious general, whose army destroys the enemies of the emperor. Some say that the precious general subdues enemies just through the power of his majesty. I have the royal possession of wisdom due to learning and contemplation. I have the wisdom gained from hearing the Buddha's words and commentaries to them and the wisdom gained from analyzing the teachings until certainty is achieved. This wisdom defeats incorrect views, which are the enemy.

Even if you are a king you need these faultless qualities that benefit beings.

The king's messenger said, "You truly follow the dharma. It is marvellous. The king told me to give you these offerings if you refused to come." He then gave Milarepa the cotton and the yellow myrobalan. Milarepa accepted the offering and recited a dedication and wishing prayer.

Some time later, Rechungpa and a pupil of Milarepa named Shengomrepa came searching for Milarepa to bring him back to Tibet. They couldn't find him until they met some hunters who said to them, "You're not real yogins. A yogin should be like Milarepa. Weapons can't pierce him, fire can't burn him, throw him in the water and he won't sink, throw him off a cliff and he'll float right back up. The king even invited him to court and he refused to go. That's what a real siddha is like." Rechungpa and Shengomrepa gave the hunters a gift, asked them where Milarepa was, and then went to him.

When they arrived, Milarepa gave Rechungpa and Shengomrepa a teaching on practice being essential and then returned to Tibet with them.

9

Entering a Yak Horn

The thirty-eighth chapter of *The Hundred Thousand Songs of Milarepa*,[53] is entitled "Entering a Yak-Horn." This story is important because it teaches that the pupil must abandon pride and show respect to the guru. This may seem at first a strange thing to do, but respect for the guru is extremely important. Only if one believes in the guru can one gain all the benefits and results of dharma practice.

It can seem suspicious when a lama like myself, seated upon a throne, is teaching people that they must have faith and devotion for the lama. But nevertheless, that is how the benefit of the dharma is obtained.

This chapter tells us that Rechungpa, Milarepa's moon-like disciple, (which means the next most important disciple after Gampopa, who was Milarepa's sun-like principal pupil) had gone to India.

One day, Milarepa realized in his meditation that Rechungpa had returned from India and was coming to see him. But he also noticed that Rechungpa had become affected by pride. Rechungpa was thinking, "My guru is of course a special person, but I've been to India twice and I've met many special gurus, and received profound instructions from them. I am no longer the same as I used to be. In the past I had to undergo many hardships in my dharma practice, but now that I am a very special lama I won't have to do that anymore."

Milarepa, aware of Rechungpa's state of mind, miraculously transferred himself into the middle of the vast plain that Rechungpa was crossing and approached him. Rechungpa thought, "I am now someone who propagates the Buddha's teachings and helps many beings. That was the reason I went to India. Now my guru has come to greet me. He has greater powers of blessing than I do, but I am more learned than he is. When I prostrate to him, I am sure that he will prostrate to me in turn."

The Story of Darmadode

Rechungpa had been given a staff by Tibupa to give to Milarepa. Tibupa, had been Marpa Lotsawa's son, Darmadode, in his previous life.

Darmadode had died quite young. This came about when he had been practicing in retreat when he saw many people going to a festival. Due to the influence of the *maras*, Darmadode heard someone say, "Why is such an important person as Darmadode not going to the festival?" Darmadode then said to his parents, "Even the old people are going to this festival, so I'm going too."

At the festival the maras caused him to have a fatal accident while he was riding a horse. Although Darmadode had received the instructions of *trong jug*, the transference of one's consciousness into a dead body, he couldn't find a human body to enter, so he entered a pigeon's body instead and flew to the Shitavana charnel-ground in India.[54] There he transferred his consciousness into the dead body of a young Brahmin, which he then reanimated. In that new body he became known as Tibupa, because *tibu* means "pigeon."

Tibupa possessed not only the instructions he had received as Darmadode, but he also passed on many instructions that he obtained in India. Due to this, he became known as "the trunk of the mantrayana tree."

Rechungpa's Shortened Life

Rechungpa had met Darmadode in India, and was receiving instructions from him, when one day Tibupa told him to go to the market place. Rechungpa met a yogin there who said, "How sad, you are such a handsome Tibetan, but you have only seven days to live!"

Rechungpa was very frightened that he was about to die and told Tibupa what the yogin had said. Tibupa said, "Don't worry, go and see Ekamatrika Siddharajni. She's a hundred and fifteen years old, but looks as if she's only sixteen. She will give you the instructions for gaining a long life."

Rechungpa went to her, received the instructions, practiced for seven days and then *Amitayus* appeared to him and asked. "How long do you want to live?" "As long as I wish!" Rechungpa answered. "You can't do that," said Amitayus, "but you're in your forty-fourth year now, and you can live until your eighty-first year," which is exactly how long Rechungpa lived for.

Returning to our story, Rechungpa had brought Tibupa's staff to Tibet, and gave it to Milarepa when they met, and then prostrated to him. Milarepa however did not prostrate to Rechungpa, contrary to Rechungpa's expectation.

Rechungpa asked, "What have you been doing while I was in India? How are the other yogins?" Milarepa, noticing signs of pride in Rechungpa, smiled and sang a song in which he said:

I am very well, because I am free from the sickness of the *five defilements* that I had suffered from throughout beginningless samsara.

Abandoning distractions, I dwell alone, independent, without attachment to anyone. I am well and happy because I live in uninhabited places that are free of worldly activities.

I am well and happy because I am free of the worries of scholarship, fame, and composing texts, and can accumulate any merit I wish.

In answer to that song, Rechungpa sang of his journey to India in which he said:

The way to India was long and dangerous. Nevertheless I underwent that hardship and achieved success. I met Tibupa and Ekamatsika Siddharajni. Also the *yidam* appeared to me and I received "the nine dharmas of the disembodied dakinis"[55] from Tibupa, and therefore I am very happy.

Now that I have met my guru again, I can offer him these nine dharmas of the disembodied dakinis, and so I am very happy.

To dispel Rechungpa's pride, Milarepa replied with a song:

Do not boast so much. I will sing you a song, and if you think it's any good, keep it in mind.

These dharmas of the disembodied dakinis are the property of the dakinis. You mustn't go around saying that you have them; their possession should be kept a secret and passed on only to a worthy disciple. If you teach these dharmas indiscriminately, the dakinis will be upset. Don't think your instructions are so special. If you do, your mind will turn bad.

If you give many high teachings, you will encounter an obstacle to your meditation. It is the arrogance of thinking, "I have accomplished so much" and it will result in abandoning a guru for a new one. Don't be like that.

Then Milarepa used his miraculous powers to run off at great speed, taking Tibupa's staff and Rechungpa's texts with him.

Rechungpa was soon exhausted trying to catch up with him, and so he called to him to stop by singing a song in which he said:

I have the teachings of the dakinis. Please read them. I have the deity-meditation of Siddharajni, which I offer to you. I have many instructions for protection, health, and countering demons, which I offer to you. Accept them and stop for moment, I'm exhausted.

Milarepa stopped and sang a song in which he said:

For one who follows the path of the dharma, the teachings of the disembodied dakinis brings neither benefit nor harm.

Tibupa has a greater connection with me than with you, and I am also a pupil of Siddharajni. I have been many times to Tibupa's dwelling place to take part in his ganachakras.

What you have to tell me is of no importance. What we need to do now is go to a solitary place in the mountains and meditate.

Rechungpa began to think negative thoughts about Milarepa, thinking, "If this had been any other lama, I would have had a great welcome party on my return from India. What kind of welcome is one old man in a cotton robe. I'm going to go back to India! My meditation practice should now be conjoined with the enjoyment of sensory pleasures."

Milarepa, being aware of Rechungpa's thoughts, pointed to a yak horn lying nearby and said, "Bring me that yak horn." Rechungpa thought, "My guru always says that he doesn't need anything, that he has no attachment for anything, but now he desires to possess this yak horn." He then said aloud to Milarepa, "What is the point of carrying such a useless thing? You can't eat it, or wear it."

Milarepa answered, "I have no attachment to it, but if I keep it, it will prove useful sometime." They then carried on walking across the great plain of Tibet that was known as Palmo Paltang. While they were still in the middle of it, black clouds gathered and they were caught in a severe hailstorm.

As the hailstones began to strike Rechungpa, without looking to see what Milarepa was doing, he hid under his cotton robe. As the hail began to lessen he wondered, "What happened to my guru?" and peeked out. There was no sign of Milarepa anywhere. "Where has he gone?" Rechungpa wondered, looking all around.

Then he heard Milarepa singing, but the sound of Milarepa's voice was coming from inside the yak horn.

Rechungpa thought, "This is the yak horn Milarepa was carrying" and tried to pick it up, but it was so heavy he couldn't move it. He looked inside and saw that Milarepa was sitting inside, singing. However Milarepa's body had not become any smaller and the yak horn had not become any larger. Milarepa sang a song:

> Rechungpa's view is like a vulture. Sometimes it's high up and sometimes it's low down. Don't run about so, your robe will be soaked. You should come inside this yak horn with me. It's very nice in here.
>
> Rechungpa is like the sun and moon, it's sometimes clear, and sometimes obscured. Rechungpa's conduct is like the wind, it's sometimes gentle, and sometimes brisk. Don't run around out there, come inside this yak horn. It's very nice in here.
>
> I've never been to India. I'm just an old man, so I sit in the back end of the narrow tip of the yak horn. You've been to India and you are a great scholar, so you should sit in the wide front end of the yak horn, at the mouth.

Rechungpa thought, "Well, who knows? There might be room for me in there," but no matter how hard he tried, he couldn't even get his hand in. Rechungpa started shivering with cold and sang into the yak horn a song in which he said:

> It is true what you say about the lack of stability in my view, meditation, and conduct. But whether my

robe is dry or soaked, you are my root guru, and I pray to you.

Milarepa came out from the yak horn and looked up into the sky. The clouds parted and the sun shone, drying Rechungpa's robe.

After sitting in this place for a little while, Milarepa said, "You didn't need to learn sorcery in India. I know how to do that. As for the dharma, I didn't go to India because I have the Six Yogas of Naropa, which are so profound that I am perfectly satisfied by having just them. But it is very good that you went to India and obtained the dharmas of the disembodied dakini as they will be needed by people in the future.

10

The Story of Gampopa

*M*ilarepa's principal disciple, who was known as his sun-like pupil, was Gampopa. The account of how Gampopa met, learned from, and practiced under Milarepa serves as an example for us. If we can practice in the same way, we can become like Gampopa. This story is found in the forty-first chapter in *The Hundred Thousand Songs of Milarepa.*[56]

Marpa Lotsawa had prophesied, on the basis of a dream that Milarepa had, that Milarepa would be one of the four "pillars," that is, one of the four main pupils who would preserve and transmit Marpa's lineage. Marpa also prophesied that Milarepa would have an unrivalled pupil who would make Marpa's lineage flourish for a long time and he would benefit countless beings. Milarepa also received a prophecy from *Vajrayogini*, who said that he would have three pupils that would be like the sun, the moon and the stars. The pupil who was like the sun was Gampopa. Gampopa was also prophesied by the Buddha in the *King of Samadhi* sutra, in the *Mahakaruna-pundarika*[57] sutra, and others, where the Buddha said that there would be a physician monk in the land of the Himalayas who would follow the Mahayana and benefit the Buddha's teachings and many beings. Gampopa is also known as Dagpo Lharje, which means "the Physician from Dagpo" in Tibetan.

Gampopa combined the teachings of the Kadampa tradition, which was one of the eight lineages of Tibetan Buddhism, with the teachings of Milarepa. So Gampopa's lineage, called the Dhagpo Kagyu, contains both an introductory path for beginners and the profound path of the Mahamudra and the Six Yogas of Naropa. From this lineage of vast and profound instructions there have been many exceptional siddhas.

From about the age of fifteen Gampopa learned many practices. As his father was a doctor, he also studied medicine. He married a very beautiful woman, but she became very sick. Even though his examination of her indicated that her vital physical elements were exhausted, she still did not die, but clung onto life. Gampopa decided that she must be clinging onto life simply out of attachment to something and said to her, "There is nowhere that is free of death. Give up your attachment to this life. If you are attached to the land, I will offer it to a temple. If you are attached to possessions, I will use them to sponsor virtuous activities."

She answered, "I don't have any attachment to land or possessions, as the things of samsara have no essence, but I want you to practice the dharma well." He promised her that he would. Then his wife died, and in accordance with his promise, he left home in order to follow the dharma.

He went to Penpo, a place to the east of Lhasa, where there were many masters of the Kadampa tradition. There he took monastic ordination and received the name Sonam Rinchen (meaning precious merit). He studied many sutra teachings, such as the *Sutralamkara* and the *Prajnaparamita*. He also studied many tantras such as the *Guhyasamaja*. He received the general

Kadampa teachings on impermanence, bodhichitta, *sending and taking practice* (Tib. *tong len*), and many other instructions from numerous lamas.

He practiced these instructions and developed great wisdom, compassion, faith and diligence. He diminished his defilements and became an excellent monk. During the day he received teachings and contemplated them and during the night he meditated, attaining many good signs. For example, he had no insects on his body, and he could pass four or five days in a state of bliss in which he did not eat but felt no hunger.

One day Gampopa had a vision in his meditation of a dark-skinned[58] yogin dressed in a cotton robe who put his hand on his head and spat upon him, and then his meditation and insight improved. He told the other monks of his experience but they said, "You are a good monk, so a vision of a yogin must be the manifestation of a Gyalpo spirit.[59] You must go to the abbot and request the empowerment of the protector Acala[60] so that its blessing will remove this obstacle to your practice." Gampopa did as his friends advised and recited mantras and prayers, but nevertheless the visions of the yogin became more frequent. Gampopa thought, "Surely this can't be a delusion caused by demons."

At that time Milarepa was teaching his pupils in the Boto Chipuk cave at Tramar. His older pupils said, "You are now quite old. If you leave us for another Buddha realm, we will need a regent to remove our obstacles, to make our practice progress, and have someone to whom patrons can make offerings so that they can accumulate merit. We need someone to whom you have transmitted the entirety of your instructions. Otherwise our lineage will have no future."

Milarepa answered, "I will examine my dreams tonight and tomorrow morning you should all assemble here." The next morning Milarepa told them, "There is an exceptional disciple who can take care of my pupils and spread the Buddha's teachings. He is a Kadampa monk who is coming from the west. I dreamt last night that this pupil brought an empty crystal vase and that I filled it with the entire contents of a golden vase, filling it to the brim. This is a good dream foretelling the future growth of the Buddha's teachings." Then Milarepa sang a song, which contains many poetical images, but the principal meaning is as follows:

> We practice the teachings of Naropa and Maitripa. You all know that they are very profound. If they are not meditated upon, there will be no profound result. But if we do meditate upon them, we can gain the full profound result.
>
> These profound instructions were obtained in India by my root guru, Marpa Lotsawa. They are the instructions that Milarepa practices. In the future I will transmit these to one who is worthy.

Meanwhile, one day when Gampopa was circumambulating he saw three beggars, who were in fact emanations of Milarepa. While Gampopa was wondering whether to speak to them or not, he heard one say, "If only we had good clothes and good food so that our stomachs were completely stuffed, we would be so happy."

Another of the beggars said, "It's not good to wish for food. If I could have a wish fulfilled, I would become like the Lord of yogins, Milarepa, whose food is meditation, whose clothing is a single cotton robe and the heat of tummo, and who meditates day and night in the Mahamudra state. When he wants to go somewhere, he just flies through the sky. I wish I could be with him, abandoning all care for this life, practicing as he does. And if that is not possible, I would wish to just see him sometimes to practice the dharma under him. That is the kind of wish you should make."

On hearing this, Gampopa felt overwhelming faith in Milarepa and thought about him well into the night. When he woke up the next morning, he prostrated himself in the direction of Milarepa and prayed to him. He then invited the beggars into his room and gave them good clothes, food, and drink. He said to them, "Yesterday you were talking about someone named Milarepa. If you can take me to him, I will give you half of all I own. And if you practice the dharma it will be very beneficial for you."

Two of the beggars said that they did not know where Milarepa was, but the older beggar said, "I know where he is. I can take you there." Gampopa made offerings and recited prayers, and when he slept that night, he dreamed that he was blowing a long horn very loudly, so that many humans and animals gathered around him. Then a woman came to him, carrying a drum and a bowl of milk. She said, "Beat this drum for the humans and give this milk to the animals." When Gampopa wondered, "How can I give milk to all these animals when I only have one bowl?" the woman said, "If you drink the milk, all these animals will obtain milk in the future."

The humans in the dream were the followers of the Hinayana who could not practice one-pointedly. Therefore their minds must be trained through the gradual path of the Kadampas. The animals were the practitioners to whom he could transmit Milarepa's instructions on Mahamudra. In order to do so, he would have to first practice these instructions himself and then he would be able to transmit them to others, greatly benefiting beings.

Gampopa, with the old beggar as his guide, set off to find Milarepa, but halfway through their journey the beggar fell ill and said, "I can go no further. I don't know exactly where Milarepa is anyway. Carry on by yourself and you are sure to find someone who will take you to him." Gampopa continued on his own, but when he had nearly reached his destination he became too weak to go any further due to a lack of food. He could only pray, "May I meet Milarepa, if not in this life, then in the next!"

That day a Kadampa monk happened to come along and came to Gampopa's aid. The monk asked him where he was going and Gampopa said, "I'm going to see Milarepa." The monk said, "I'm going to see him too." So they travelled on together and reached the area where Milarepa was staying.

Gampopa met one of Milarepa's female patrons. She said to him, "You must have come from central Tibet to meet Milarepa, I know because Milarepa has already said that you are coming." Gampopa thought, "I must be a worthy pupil if he knows that I am coming," and became somewhat proud. But then Milarepa refused to see Gampopa for two weeks to eliminate that pride. At least, that is what is described in the text, but since Gampopa was a special being who was prophesied in the sutras by the Buddha, it is not possible that he could have been subject to pride. Gampopa must have manifested this pride in order to demonstrate to future generations that pride is something to be avoided on meeting the guru.

When Gampopa finally met Milarepa, Gampopa offered him sixteen ounces of gold in a mandala offering. He also made a request that Milarepa tell his life-story. Milarepa sat with his eyes half-closed for a little while and then took a pinch of gold from the center of the mandala offering and scattered it into the air, saying, "I offer this to you, Marpa Lotsawa." Milarepa had been drinking beer from a skull bowl. He handed this to Gampopa, saying, "Drink this." Gampopa hesitated,[61] but Milarepa said, "Don't think so much, drink!"

Gampopa thought, "This lama is omniscient. He knows whatever is in my mind. So this must be a very auspicious thing to do," and he drank the beer to the last drop, which was indeed very auspicious. Milarepa said, "That you had faith in me and have come here is a wonderful thing, so I shall tell you the story of my life." Milarepa then sang a song:

> Naropa and Maitripa's instructions contain all that is taught by the Buddhas in the three times. Marpa Lotsawa possessed these instructions. I felt faith in him on just hearing his name and I received all these instructions from him.
>
> Marpa Lotsawa told me, "This is the age of degeneration; life is short and uncertain. There are many causes of death, therefore do not make the error in believing the instructions are the mere acquisition of knowledge because practice is their essence." Due to the kindness of the guru, that has been my view. I meditated upon the fear of death; I meditated with diligence in caves; my meditation transformed my thoughts and wrong views into merit.
>
> The three poisons of anger, desire, and ignorance appear to be the powerful causes of the accumulation of negative karma. But when their essence is seen to be emptiness, those poisons are recognized to be the dharmakaya, sambhogakaya, and nirmanakaya.
>
> The blessings, experiences and realizations of Naropa and Maitripa are transmitted through the

lineage to the worthy pupil. I shall give their profound instructions to you. Practice them correctly, and spread the Buddha's teachings for the benefit of beings.

I have no need for the gold you have offered me. Gold does not agree with this old man. If you want to practice the dharma properly, observe my conduct and my practice, and do as I do.

The monk who had come with Gampopa came to receive a blessing from Milarepa. Milarepa asked the monk to offer him everything that he had in order to receive a blessing. The monk said that he didn't have anything to give. But Milarepa said, "You have a lot of gold concealed about your body, so your statement that you don't have anything is truly wonderful. If you have no faith you are incapable of receiving a blessing. If you have no faith, the instructions that you receive will not benefit you. Your inner thoughts are of going to Nepal to do business, so that is the best thing for you to do. I will pray that you meet no obstacles."

Gampopa thought, "This lama knows what people think. It is impossible to deceive him. I will have good control over my mind and think carefully before I ask him anything. He truly is a Buddha."

Milarepa asked Gampopa, "Have you received any empowerments? What instructions have you been given? What practices have you done?" Gampopa answered Milarepa's questions and described his success in meditation, but Milarepa just laughed and said, "You can't get oil by grinding sand, you have to use mustard seeds. These empowerments you have received are useless for seeing the true nature of your mind. If you meditate on my tummo instructions you will see the true nature of your mind."

Milarepa then gave Gampopa the *Vajravarahi* empowerment, using a sindhura[62] mandala. Then he gave Gampopa the instructions and Gampopa put them into practice.

Gampopa had good experiences and realizations, and had many thoughts on view, meditation, and conduct. He asked Milarepa to explain them, and in answer, Milarepa sang a spiritual song describing the view, meditation, conduct, commitment and result, in terms of the true nature as the basis of the path:

The ultimate view is to look at your own mind.

What does Milarepa mean by that line? If one has never practiced that may seem a simple thing to do, but this is the ultimate view in Vajrayana practice. The sutra tradition teaches emptiness and selflessness which are to be understood through analysis by searching vainly for the self from the crown of the head to one's toenails. Deduction brings conviction that the body and all phenomena have no reality. This is the understanding of emptiness. Meditation upon this conviction will then lead to the ultimate goal. The sutra path is therefore called "the path of deduction." The Vajrayana, however, does not use deduction, but uses the direct perception of emptiness, of the true nature of phenomena. So it is called "the path of direct experience."

The true nature cannot be seen directly in outer phenomena, but, by looking into one's own mind and seeing that the mind cannot be found.[63] The mind is the embodiment of emptiness, the essence of emptiness, but throughout beginningless time we have never looked at our own mind. The emptiness of the mind is not a vacuity but a clarity.[64] It is a mistake to try and find emptiness other than in the mind.

To illustrate this there is a story of a man who had a jewel inset into his forehead. Whenever he was tired the skin on his head sagged. One day when he was very exhausted and the skin sagged and covered the jewel completely. The man felt his forehead and thought he had lost the jewel, and ran around anxiously trying to find it, only becoming more tired in the process, so that the jewel was more deeply hidden.

In the same way, Milarepa says, "to search for the true nature anywhere other than our own mind, is like a blind monster looking for gold."

Milarepa then described meditation to Gampopa in a single line of song:

> The ultimate practice is not to consider lethargy and
> excitability as faults.

A beginner of meditation, of course, does need to work on eliminating lethargy and excitability in meditation, but the nature of lethargy and excitability is the nature of the mind and this nature never changes. If you see these two qualities of mind as obstacles or faults, you will not be able to see the essence of the mind. Therefore you should not attempt to eliminate them, which would as Milarepa says "be as pointless as lighting a candle in the daylight." Next, Milarepa described conduct:

> The ultimate action is to cease to accept and reject.

The usual Buddhist practice is to accept what is positive and to reject what is negative. In terms of the true nature there should be no adoption of good actions or abandonment of negative actions.

Whatever arises in the mind has the ultimate nature of the clarity and emptiness of the mind, so we should not think, "this is good and has to be cultivated or this is bad and has to be rejected." If we attempt to adopt and reject, we will be like a fly struggling in a cobweb, which only binds itself tighter the more it does.

Next Milarepa describes commitment:

The ultimate discipline is to rest in the ultimate view.

Discipline is usually made by promising to keep all our commitments and vows. But remaining in the realization of the true nature of our mind is truly keeping the commitment. If we strive to maintain a commitment that is other than the mind, we will always fail. It is just as Milarepa says, "we can't stop water's natural propensity to flow downward." Next Milarepa describes the accomplishment or result of our practice:

The ultimate accomplishment is full conviction in one's mind.

The ultimate result is the true nature of the mind manifest. If one seeks a result that does not already exist, that would be like as Milarepa says, "a frog jumping up into the sky," which is inevitably going to fall back onto the ground. The result can only be found in the mind itself.

The Buddha's wisdom is described as "the sudden result" even in the sutra tradition, because the wisdom spontaneously appears as soon as the defilements are eliminated without having to be created. In the Vajrayana tradition, the result is described as the manifestation of the true nature of one's mind. This nature is primordially present, but unrecognized, within all beings. Once the nature of the mind is recognized, the ultimate result is attained.

In the next verse Milarepa describes the guru:

The ultimate guru is one's mind.

On the relative level one has a root guru whose instructions one follows. On the ultimate level the guru is one's mind. If one can look at and question one's own mind, the instructions of the ultimate guru will be received. If one seeks a guru that is other than the mind, it is as Milarepa says, "trying to leave one's mind" which is impossible. All appearances are nothing other than one's mind, so there is no greater guru than the true nature of the mind.

On hearing this song, Gampopa felt great faith. He then meditated with diligence practicing the tummo meditation. On the first night, his body filled with warmth and bliss. At dawn he fell asleep briefly and when he woke up his body was cold as stone.

After seven days of meditation he had a vision of the five Buddhas of the *five Buddha families*. He thought this was very important and told Milarepa. Milarepa said, "If you press your eyes you see an illusion of there being two moons. In the same way, the particular movement of airs in your body caused your experience, which was neither good nor bad. Just carry on with your meditation.

11

Victory over the Four Maras

I will conclude this introduction to the songs of Milarepa with this sixtieth chapter[65] that describes victory over the maras. This is very auspicious from the Tibetan point of view. The Buddha taught that there were four maras: the divine mara (Skt. *devaputra-mara*), the disturbing emotion mara (Skt. *klesha-mara*), the aggregate mara (Skt. *skandha-mara*), and the death mara (Skt. *matyupati-mara*). They cause obstacles, bring suffering, and prevent the attainment of liberation.

The "divine mara" is traditionally portrayed as a beautiful and attractive being. This mara represents the attachment to the sensory pleasures of samsara, which seems very beautiful at the time, but from the ultimate point of view, these attachments lead people astray and create an obstacle to liberation and omniscience. Therefore it is called the "divine mara."

The "mara of defilement," or the disturbing emotion mara, is the attachment to a self, which leads to the defilements of ignorance, anger, and desire. They appear within our mind and cause the accumulation of negative karma, which results in future suffering. This mara is traditionally portrayed as an old, weak Brahmin who doesn't have long to live because it is a delusion, without any solid basis, and therefore easy to eliminate. As soon as the truth is realized, delusion ceases to exist.

The "mara of the five aggregates" is next. When there are the aggregates or skandhas (form, sensation, recognition, mental events and consciousnesses), there is samsara. Until the true nature of these aggregates is realized, there is suffering. This mara is traditionally portrayed as a physically powerful being, because the skandhas are an actual presence, and their true nature is more difficult to realize than that of the defilements.

The "mara who is the Lord of Death" is death itself. At death we must leave all the activities of our life, and we feel afraid. Death will be a cause of suffering for as long as we remain in samsara. This mara is traditionally portrayed as black and terrifying, because it is brings impermanence and fear.

The way to eliminate these four maras is to practice the dharma and to realize the true nature of phenomena.

In this chapter Milarepa sings of his own victory over the maras, beginning with a song that describes the need to escape from samsara. Later it is told that Milarepa was blown over a precipice by a wind and was seen to be impaled upon a tree. His students were mortified until Milarepa showed them his body to be unharmed, without any wound at all. He then sang them a song:

> The wind made me fall, and an inanimate tree harmed my body causing me unendurable agony. However, the dakinis healed me so that I was healed from all injury.

Another time, Milarepa's students were with him on top of a very high rock when he fell off. They thought he must have died and passed into nirvana and went down to recover his body. But when they reached the bottom, Milarepa was still alive and laughed at them. When they asked him what had happened, Milarepa replied with a song:

> The vulture of union spreads its wings. When the vulture of the union of emptiness and clarity spreads its wings, it does not fly using only one of them. When we meditate, the wisdom of the emptiness of phenomena alone is not enough, and the wisdom of clarity alone is not enough to cause the realization of the true nature of phenomena.
>
> The essence of clarity is emptiness. Emptiness, the unreality of phenomena, is not a voidness but has clarity. This is "the union of space and wisdom." The realization of this union will enable us to reach liberation from samsara.

This is what Milarepa meant by "the vulture of union spreading its wings."

> The flight was from the peak of Tramar,[66] The landing was in the ravine below. I played a joke upon my followers.

Milarepa, through a miracle, flew from the top of Tramar and then landed on the ground below. Then he explained:

> There was a purpose to the joke: The wings of the union of wisdom and emptiness realized the true nature so that there is freedom from the obscurations caused by the defilements and the obscurations to

knowledge.[67] Then liberation from both samsara and nirvana is demonstrated. Then there is the peace of emptiness united with perfect bliss.

Another time, Milarepa and his disciples were at the foot of a rocky cliff. One of his disciples said to him, "You shouldn't stay here, it's too dangerous." But he did and a little later there was a rockslide. Milarepa stared and pointed at the falling rocks and they immediately scattered into different directions, without harming him. His students returned certain that Milarepa had been injured. When they arrived, he sang them a song:

This yogin's body is like a flower. The avalanche of rocks was like a murderer wanting to kill a flower. A dakini appeared on my right and left so that the rocks did not fall upon me. I am not afraid of the maras, they could never cause an obstacle to me.

The students asked, "You have been in an avalanche, fallen off a precipice, and been impaled upon a tree, without being harmed. How is this possible?"

Milarepa answered, "My realization of the true nature of phenomena has made my body as insubstantial as a rainbow and it has transformed my defilements into wisdoms. My certain knowledge that all phenomena are unborn has blown away the eight worldly dharmas.[68] This is a sign that the four maras are ashamed, have lost their confidence and are powerless."

His pupils then asked, "Does this mean that you have conquered the four maras?" And Milarepa replied, "Yes, there has been victory over the maras. For the next thirteen successions of my lineage, the maras will not be able to cause any obstacles to its practitioners."

A *tantrika* student arrived from central Tibet, and Sebenrepa asked him what siddhas were in that region. The tantrika replied, "There are many siddhas there, and they are served by non-human beings."

Milarepa said, "That doesn't make anyone a siddha." Sebenrepa then asked Milarepa, "Do non-human beings serve you?" Milarepa replied that they did and sang a song:

> The food of *samadhi* that is served to me is inexhaustible, like the treasury of space. I am free of thoughts and feelings of hunger and thirst. This is a service rendered to me by dakinis, but I do not think of it as a siddhi. It is only an experience within meditation, not the ultimate siddhi[69] of realizing the true nature of phenomena.

The tantrika said that there were masters in the central region that had seen the face of the yidam. But Milarepa said, "Just seeing the yidam's face is of no benefit." Then he sang:

> Due to my meditation on the instructions I have received from Marpa Lotsawa, I have seen the nature of the mind. This dispelled the darkness of ignorance from my mind. All the dakinis revealed their faces to me, but there are no faces in the true nature, which contains no objects of perception.
>
> I have seen the yidam's face, but only the root guru's teachings are important. I have attained the

general siddhis but the realization of the true nature transcends them.

The tantrika then asked, "Can you give me an example of what you mean by 'seeing the nature of the mind'?" In answer Milarepa sang a song:

The mind has no true reality and is therefore unborn and unceasing. In every instant the mind gives birth to thoughts. But if you see the nature of the mind, you know that it has no reality, and has never been born. You cannot find the mind's location and so it is unborn.

There is no example that can be given to depict the unborn mind, because nothing resembles it. It has no birth or cessation. Only what is born comes to an end. When you realize the nature of the mind you know that nothing can serve as an example for it, except for the mind itself. Then the example and the meaning will be the same.

You can't describe the nature of the mind in the way that you can describe an outer object as white or red. You can't say that the nature of the mind exists or that it doesn't exist. The mind is inconceivable, beyond deduction, beyond the scope of speech, but due to the blessing of the root guru and the lineage gurus, you can see it for yourself.

Notes

1. See L. P. Lhalungpa *The Life of Milarepa*. Published by Shambhala Publications, 1985.
2. For more information on Tsang Nyön Heruka see *The Life of Marpa the Translator*. Boston: Shambhala, 1986 pages xx-xxiv.
3. Tib. *dbus*. This is the region of central Tibet that had Lhasa as its capital.
4. This is the region of central Tibet that had Gyantse as its capital.
5. In the Vajrayana, there are two paths – *drol lam* and *thap lam* – that are generally followed simultaneously or alternately by the practitioner. *Drol lam,* the path of liberation, is what sometimes we refer to as formless meditation and includes Mahamudra. In this approach to meditation one relates to the mind in terms of the awareness aspect of mind.

   Thap lam, the path of means or method, includes all tantric practices employing visualization, mantras, mandalas, yogas such as *the Six Dharmas of Naropa* or the *Six Dharmas of Niguma,* etc. These practices relate to mind in terms of the energy aspect of mind. By properly integrating the distorted karmic energies of one's mind, one brings about the same enlightened awareness that is reached as the fruition of the formless meditation approach of the path of liberation. The virtue of the path of liberation is that it tends to be smoother, while the path of means is that it tends to be faster; therefore, they make a good complement to each other.

Neither path can be practiced properly – and in the case of the path of means it would be dangerous to do so – without the guidance of a qualified tantric master. – *Lama Tashi Namgyal*

6. These four thoughts also called the four ordinary foundations are more fully explained in Thrangu Rinpoche's *The Four Foundations of Buddhist Practice*. Namo Buddha Publications.

7. All meditation can be divided into the two categories of tranquillity meditation (Shamatha) and insight meditation (Vipashyana). Vipashyana in turn can be divided into the Vipashyana of the sutra tradition and the Vipashyana of the Mahamudra tradition. In the sutra tradition there is analytical Vipashyana and placement meditation. In the Mahamudra or tantric tradition, Vipashyana is based on the direct pointing out of the nature of mind and the nature of things by a fully qualified and experienced holder of the Mahamudra lineage. – *Lama Tashi Namgyal*

8. One of the greatest lamas of the nineteenth century (1820 - 1892) and one of the most important tertons. He was considered to be a body emanation of Jigme Lingpa. He was heavily involved in the development of the non-sectarian Rime-movement. The goal of which was for the practitioner to attain complete mastery of the teachings of all the lineages, so as to then be able to give each of his students the precise teaching to fit their individual needs.

9. Gampopa had previously been a great *bodhisattva* and at the time of Shakyamuni Buddha had taken rebirth as a monk. At that time Lord Shakyamuni in the *King of Samadhi Sutra* prophesied that Gampopa would again take rebirth in a distant land as a monk named Tzodzad. The name Tzodzad indicated that the monk would be a doctor, so this prophecy can be seen to point to the case of Gampopa, who was born in Tibet, became a doctor, and later took monastic ordination at a *Kadampa* monastery. This prophecy of the Buddha is more fully described in Thrangu Rinpoche's *The King of Samadhi* which is one of the few sutras which directly discusses Mahamudra meditation. – *Khenchen Thrangu Rinpoche*

10. The lineage from Dorje Chang to Gampopa is referred to as the "general" Kagyu lineage, because it is the source of all Kagyu traditions. Dusum Khyenpa, founded the Kamtzang Karma Kagyu tradition. Tsultrim Nyingpo received the lineage of Gampopa's monastery, Daglha Gompa, and founded the tradition known as the Tshelpa Kagyu through his disciple Tsondru Trakpa. Baram Dharma Wangchuk travelled north to Baram, settled there his tradition became known as the Baram Kagyupa. Khampa Dorgyal, the most expansive teacher of the group, also went north, found a place called Phagmodru in the forest of Samantabhadra, and built a monastery there. He became known as Phagmo Drupa, named from the place where he built his monastery. His tradition became known as the Phagmodru Kagyupa.

The Kamtzang, Tshelpa, Baram, and Phagmodru subsects are called the four "primary traditions" of the Kagyu because they originated from the four main disciples of Gampopa.

Phagmo Drupa, from the vastness of the teachings he had collected, gave different instructions to various and numerous disciples, and in doing so gave rise to eight different traditions. These are the Drigung, Taklung, Yabzang, Shugseb, Marpa, Yelpa, Throphupa and the Drukpa Kagyu sects, which are collectively known as the eight "secondary lineages." From all of these lineages came a large number of siddhas and incarnated lamas.

Due primarily to the efforts of their early teachers, of the eight "secondary traditions," three became especially prominent: Drigung Kyobpa Jigten Gonpo's Drigung lineage; Taklung Thangpa Trashi Pal's Taklungpa lineage; and the Drukpa Kagyupa lineage, which took its name from the Namdruk Gon Monastery founded by Tsangpa Gyarepa, a disciple of Lingchen Repa, and from which came a great many siddhas. – *Khenchen Thrangu Rinpoche*

11. Garma Chang: *The Hundred Thousand Songs of Milarepa.* Boston: Shambhala Publications, 1962. Pages 1-10. In Garma Chang's book this chapter is entitled *The Tale of Red Rock Jewel Valley.*

12. Blessing is the process by which one individual introduces some of their accumulated merit into another's "stream of being." The ability to bestow blessing depends on the donor's degree of spiritual attainment and on the recipient's faith. The donor is usually the root-guru, whose blessing is said to contain that of all the sources of refuge combined. Although future experiences are largely shaped by present actions, the root-guru's blessing can partially modify this. That is, it can create conditions favourable to the maturation of any religious pre-dispositions our past actions may have generated, giving us the inspiration and energy we require to begin practising. In this way, unless our acts have been extremely unwholesome, the guru's blessing can help us overcome conflicting emotions and other obstacles. Thus the guru's blessing helps us realize the Buddha-potential we all possess.

13. The word is derived from the Sanskrit acharya or a religious master.

14. The word deity is often used rather broadly, here it is referring to beings that are not enlightened. Local deities are beings who inhabit specific places, although they are not visible to most humans they can be quite powerful and can cause harm or obstacles to one if they are not respected; just as we would get upset and angry if someone violated our home, we should consider and respect the home or territory of others, even if we cannot visibly see them. Therefore Buddhist practitioners often make offerings to local deities for good circumstances.

15. In the Sanskrit *bodhi* means "awakened" or "enlightened" and *chitta* means "mind," so bodhichitta means awakened mind. The generation of bodhichitta is based on the altruistic wish to bring about the welfare, and ultimately the total liberation, of all sentient beings from all forms of suffering. What distinguishes bodhichitta from the ordinary compassionate aspirations to benefit others shared by all people of good will is the recognition that one cannot ultimately fulfill these aspirations until one has attained the state of mental purification and liberation of Buddhahood, which is the

source of all positive qualities, including the omniscience that can see, individual by individual, the causes of suffering and the causes and path of liberation from suffering. This understanding gives rise at some point to the initial generation of the aspiration to attain the state of Buddhahood in order to liberate all sentient beings from suffering and to establish them all in states of happiness. This is called bodhichitta of aspiration, which must be followed by what is called the bodhichitta of application, which is the training in loving-kindness, compassion, the six paramitas or transcendent perfections, etc., which lead to the accomplishment of Buddhahood. Aspiration bodhichitta and application bodhichitta are both included in the term relative bodhichitta. Ultimate bodhichitta is direct insight into the ultimate nature. This state of primordial awareness *is* compassion and loving-kindness and gives rise spontaneously and without preconception to compassionate activity.
– *Lama Tashi Namgyal*

16. This is *The Song of Realization* in Garma Chang's *Hundred Thousand Songs of Milarepa*, p. 6-7. Also in *Rain of Wisdom*, p. 202-204.
17. Garma Chang. *The Hundred Thousand Songs of Milarepa*. Page 23-37.
18. Garma Chang. *The Hundred Thousand Songs of Milarepa*. Pages 11-22.
19. Garma Chang translates this as eighteen days in *The Hundred Thousand Songs*. The Tibetan is literally "eighteen days and nights" which is explained later in the song as nine daytimes and nighttimes.
20. In Tibetan medicine and meditation the body contains numerous subtle channels (Skt. *nadi*, Tib. *tsa*) which are not anatomical in nature, but more like channels in acupuncture. There are thousands of channels but the three main channels are the central channel, which runs roughly along the spinal column and the left and right channels either side of this. *Prana* is the energy, or "wind," moving through the nadis. As is said, "Mind consciousness rides the horse of prana on the pathways of the nadis. The *bindu* is mind's nourishment."

Because of dualistic thinking, prana enters the left and right channels. This divergence of energy in the subtle body corresponds to the mental activity that falsely distinguishes between subject and object and leads to karmically determined activity. Through yogic practice, the pranas can be brought into the central channel and therefore transformed into wisdom-prana. Then the mind can recognize its fundamental nature, realizing all dharmas as unborn [empty].

21. Kleshas, in Sanskrit means "pain, distress, and torment." This was translated as "afflictions" which is the closest English word to what causes distress. However, the Tibetan word for kleshas is *nyon mong* and these almost always refer to passion, anger, ignorance, jealousy, and pride which are actually negative or disturbing emotions so we prefer the translation negative or disturbing emotion since "afflictions" imply some kind of disability. *The Great Tibetan Dictionary* for example defines *nyon mong* as, "mental events that incite one to non-virtuous actions and cause one's being to be very unpeaceful."

22. Garma C. C. Chang: *The Hundred Thousand Songs of Milarepa*: "Challenge from a Wise Demoness," p. 38-57.

23. Tib. *srin-mo*. One of the many types of local Tibetan deities. In translations from the Sanskrit they are equated with the Indian rakshasa demons. A Rock-Sinmo, is described in Tibetan folklore as the original female ancestor of the Tibetan race – the result of her union with a monkey. These two ancestral creatures became identified as emanations of Tara and Avalokiteshvara.

24. In Tibetan medicine madness is considered to be caused by an influx of subtle airs into the heart. The application of a golden needle is a Tibetan medical method, now very rarely used, which is analogous to Chinese acupuncture.

25. Latencies (Skt. *vasana*, Tib. *bakchak*) These latent imprints that enter the eighth (ground) consciousness come through the seventh (afflicted) consciousness. These imprints are not apparently the

experience itself, but are described more like dormant seeds that are away from soil, water, and sunlight. These imprints are either positive, negative, or neutral depending upon whether they came from a positive, negative, or neutral thought or action. These imprints are then activated with experience and thus help create our impression of the solidity of the world. There are actually several kinds of latencies: latencies which are associated with external sensory experiences, latencies which give rise to the dualistic belief of "I" and "other," and positive and negative latencies due to our actions which cause us to continue to revolve around and around in samsara. It should also be pointed out that different schools of Buddhism treated these latencies differently.

26. With regard to the eight consciousnesses, the first five are called the "consciousnesses of the five gates." The gates are the five senses: eye ear, nose, tongue, and body. They are called gates because they seem to be the gates by means of which your mind encounters that which is outside your body. These five consciousnesses operating through the five senses or five gates experience their objects directly. The eye consciousness actually sees shapes and colors, the ear consciousness actually detects or experiences sounds, and so on. It is direct experience, therefore these consciousnesses are non-conceptual and do not generate any thoughts about the characteristics of what they experience; they do not conceptually recognize the things that they perceive or experience.

That which thinks about what is experienced by the five senses and which conceptually recognizes them as such and such, and conceives of them as good and bad, in short that which thinks period, is the sixth consciousness, the mental consciousness. The mental consciousness does not work with or appear on the basis of a specific sense organ like the other five. It inhabits the body in a general way and it is that which thinks. The fundamental distinction between it and the others is that the five sense consciousnesses, since they engage only in the direct experience of their objects, can only experience the present. For example, the eye consciousness only sees what is there now. It does not see what was there in the past. It does not see what will be there in the future. This is also true of the ear consciousness and so on. Not only can they not think about the past or the future, they do not even conceptualise or think about the present.

The sixth consciousness on the other hand can and does think about things. The sixth consciousness thinks of the past, both the distant and recent past. But while it is capable of thinking it is not capable of directly experiencing things the way that the sense consciousnesses do. It generates a generality or abstraction on the basis of the things that are experienced by the five sense consciousnesses. This means that when the five sense consciousnesses experience something, it becomes an object of thought for the sixth consciousness, not in the form of what is actually experienced but in the form of a conceptual generality or generalization or abstraction that is created by the sixth consciousness as a duplicate or replica of what was experienced by that particular sense consciousness. For example, when I look at the glass that is on the table in front of me, my eyes directly see that glass, but my sixth consciousness, my mental consciousness does not directly see it. It generates a generality or abstraction based upon what my eyes have seen, that it recognizes, that it thinks about, thinks of as good or bad, or having such and such shape and so on.

Those six consciousnesses are relatively easy to detect or observe because they are vivid in their manifestation or function. The other two consciousnesses are less easy to observe. For one thing the six consciousnesses start and stop in their operation. They are generated by certain conditions and when those conditions are no longer present they temporarily stop functioning. Therefore the six consciousnesses are called "inconstant" consciousnesses. They are not constantly there. They are generated as they arise. The other two consciousnesses are called "constant" consciousnesses. Not only are they constant, which means that they are always operating, but they are also much less observable.

The seventh consciousness is called the "afflicted consciousness." This refers to the subtle or most basic level of mental affliction or *klesha*. Specifically, the afflicted consciousness is the most subtle level of fixation on a self that is unfluctuatingly present even when one is asleep. When sometimes you have a sense of self and you think "I," that is not an operation of the seventh consciousness. That is the sixth consciousness thinking. The seventh consciousness is present until you attain the first *bodhisattva level* and so on. Although it is not directly observable itself, it is the basis for all coarse fixation on a self and therefore for all coarse kleshas.

The eighth consciousness is called the "alaya vijnana" or "ground consciousness." It is called the ground because it is the basis for the arising of all other types of consciousness. It is that fundamental clarity of consciousness or cognitive lucidity of consciousness that has been there from the beginning. Being the capacity for conscious experience it is the ground for the arising of eye consciousness, ear consciousness, etc. It is, like the seventh, constantly present, constantly operating, and it persists until the attainment of final awakening or Buddhahood.

Along with the eight consciousnesses there is something else that is often mentioned. This is called the "immediate mind." The immediate mind is not a separate consciousness. It is the function of the impure mind that links the operations of one consciousness to another. It is that impulse or force of habit that causes the six consciousnesses to arise from the ground of the all basis and the afflicted consciousness. It is that which causes the mental consciousness to arise on the basis of a sense perception and so on. It is an identifiable function of the impure mind, but is not in itself a separate consciousness, therefore there are only eight types of impure consciousness. It is not considered to be a ninth. – *Khenchen Thrangu Rinpoche*

When we, as ordinary beings, hit a rock it is hard and hurts because of our latencies. However, Milarepa as will be seen in later stories has mastered or transformed the eight consciousness and its latencies so he can put his hand right through a rock because it is actually empty. This is much more fully explained in Thrangu Rinpoche's *Transcending Ego*, Namo Buddha Publications.

27. This refers to things being empty of inherent nature or *shunyata*. However, emptiness is inseparable from luminosity (Tib. *salwa*) and therefore this is not a blank voidness like the complete absence of something.

28. The failure of the mind to recognize its own true nature is what is meant by the term *ma rigpa*, or ignorance, the first level of delusion, obscuration or defilement in the mind. As a result of this ignorance, there arises in the mind the imputation of an "I" and an "other," (the other being something that is conceived as) something that is other than the mind. This dualistic clinging, something that we have had throughout beginningless time and that never stops (until enlightenment), is the second level of obscuration, the obscuration of habits (habitual tendency).

Based upon this dualistic clinging arise the three root mental afflictions: mental darkness (variously rendered by translators as ignorance, bewilderment, confusion, etc.), desire, and aggression. Based upon these three afflictions there arise some 84,000 various mental afflictions enumerated by the Buddha, all of which together comprise the third level of obscuration, called the obscuration of mental afflictions (variously rendered as klesha, emotional affliction, conflicting emotions, etc). Under the influence of these, we perform actions that are obscured in their nature, which result in the fourth level of obscuration, called the obscuration of actions or karma. – *Khabje Kalu Rinpoche*

29. Garma Chang. *The Hundred Thousand Songs of Milarepa*. "The Song of a Yogi's Joy," p. 74-87.

30. The first recognition of the nature of mind, which is brought about

in the student's experience through the intervention of the lama whether during a teaching, a ritual ceremony, or guided meditation becomes the basis for the student's subsequent practice of dharma, the purpose of which is to enable the student to become accustomed and habituated to experiencing the world in the manner first pointed out. When through the practice of the path, the student's experience reaches the ineffable fruition of Buddhahood, he or she is said to have fully realized the nature of mind. – *Lama Tashi Namgyal*

31. Garma Chang. *The Hundred Thousand Songs of Milarepa.* p. 136-149.

32. When you talk about guru in the Mahamudra lineage, there is the pure (dharmakaya) aspect of the guru, the distance lineage gurus, and the close lineage gurus. The distance lineage gurus start with the Lord Buddha and extend in a continuous, unbroken succession of enlightened masters and students all the way down to the Karmapa. We call that the distance lineage because it goes all the way back to the Buddha Shakyamuni.

There is the close lineage of Mahamudra as well. That lineage begins with the Buddha Vajradhara who bestowed Mahamudra teachings on the Bodhisattva Lodro Rinchen, which teachings then come down to Tilopa and Naropa. In the case of the great masters who received Mahamudra lineage transmissions directly from the Buddha Vajradhara, those transmissions happened a long time after Prince Siddhartha's paranirvana. The physical Buddha, the historical Buddha Shakyamuni, Prince Siddhartha, was at the time no longer in physical Prince Siddhartha form. What happened was that first these great masters received the teachings of the Buddha and the Buddha's disciples through " distance lineages," and they practiced them. Through their practice they attained realization. As part of their realization the Buddha manifested to them, but not as Prince Siddhartha, as Buddha Vajradhara. So, Buddha, the sambhogakaya of the Buddha, and the nirmanakaya of the Buddha, which is Prince Siddhartha in our case. The Buddha Vajradhara means all in one – the ever present Buddha, the timeless Buddha.

Then the Buddha Vajradhara transmitted directly to certain great masters, but only as a result of the realization of the teachings they had already received from their masters, whose teachings started with the historical Buddha. In this way, the Mahamudra lineage and many Vajrayana Buddhist lineages actually have distance lineage as well as close lineage. – *Tai Situ Rinpoche*

33. Dharmakaya, sambhogakaya, and nirmanakaya. Fully enlightened beings, Buddhas, and their manifestations are often understood by way of the three kayas: The dharmakaya is enlightenment itself, wisdom beyond any reference point which can only be perceived by other enlightened beings; The sambhogakaya, often called the enjoyment body, manifests in the pure lands which can only be seen by advanced bodhisattvas; and the nirmanakaya which can be seen by ordinary beings as in the case of the historical Buddha, but this can also be any type of being or relative appearance to assist ordinary beings.

34. Tib. *chö* (spelled *gcod*) Apparently originally spelt *spyod*, as in this verse and in Paldarbum's question, short *spyod-yul* as the translation of the Sanskrit *gocara*.

35. This is commonly but not always pronounced "pai" in Tibet. "Phat" practice, common in tantric incantations, for cutting ego, involves saying the Sanskrit syllable Phat. It is used as a means of cutting distracting thoughts and to arouse the consciousness from drowsiness occurring in meditation. In applying it, the yogi first concentrates on the thought-flow, drowsiness, apparitions, or whatever hindrances appear, and then suddenly shouts "pai!" with all their strength. By doing this the hindrances are eventually eliminated. – *Garma Chang.*

36. The point of direct arrival here is an aspect of that which distinguishes between the Mahamudra approach and the approach using inferential reasoning. If we are attempting to use inferential reasoning to uncover the ultimate nature of absolute truth, then there is no direct arrival involved, because the process consists of considering what there is and gradually generating confidence in its ultimate

nature as absolute truth. In the Mahamudra approach, however, there is a direct arrival or leap. What we are leaping past is conceptual consideration altogether, and what we are leaping into is the direct experience of the nature of our own mind. So, there is no consideration or analysis or labelling of substantiality, insubstantiality and so forth – we are simply directly looking at the nature of our mind, directly experiencing it, and thereby directly meditating upon it. – *Khenchen Thrangu Rinpoche*

37. This refers to the shaving of one's hair when taking ordination.

38. The display of miracles, such as leaving imprints in rocks, arises from the samadhi recognizing that all phenomena are uncreated and are, in fact, illusory. Whatever is required to benefit beings can be magically manifested out of the samadhi realizing this emptiness. – *Khenchen Thrangu Rinpoche*

39. Garma Chang. *The Hundred Thousand Songs of Milarepa.* p. 215-223.

40. Gandhamadana. Tib. *spos ngad ldan* meaning "aromatic" because traditional Indian accounts describe a fragrant forest on its slopes. It is described in the Abhidharma as being at the source of the Ganges and Brahmaputra, and as the site of the wish-fulfilling jambu tree. Anavatapta. Tib. *ma dros pa* meaning "unwarmed" suggesting a cold lake.

41. The Bonpo religion was present within Tibet before the introduction of Buddhism, and has developed and continued up to the present time.

42. Tib. *bya rgod phung po'i ri* which means "The Vulture-peak Mountain" which is at the capital of Maghada where the Buddha often resided and taught the Prajnaparamita sutras.

43. The Bon tradition circumambulates sacred places counter-clockwise, while Buddhists always go clockwise.

44. Tib. *rdzu-'phrul phug.* A temple has been built around this rock shelter. Zutrul Puki is on the southeastern side of Kailash on the final stage of the usual circumambulation of the mountain.

45. Garma Chang. *The Hundred Thousand Songs of Milarepa.* p. 287-295.
46. Tib. *snyi shangs gur rta.* Nyishang or Nyeshang is the area that is now called Manang, which lies to the east of the Kaligandaki river, to the west of the Maryadikola river, and south east of the Nepalese kingdom of Mustang.
47. Mön is a generic name used by Tibetans at that time for areas from Lhahul in the west to Tawang in the east and inhabited by non-Tibetan, Tibeto-burman peoples. It has also been used for Bhutan, and the king of Bhaktapur and Patan is referred to in the chapter heading as the king of Mön.
48. Garma Chang. *The Hundred Thousand Songs of Milarepa.* p. 275-286.
49. The text has Yerang, the name for Patan at that time.
50. The text has Khakhom, the name of Bhatgaon i.e. Bhaktapur at that time.
51. Tibetan *aru* and Sanskrit *arura*. The yellow or chebulic myrobalan or *Terminalia Chebula.*
52. The Buddha's teachings occurred in three important phases, known as the three *dharmachakras* or three turnings of the wheel of dharma. The first turning includes the teachings common to all traditions, those of the Four Noble Truths, the Eight-fold Path, selflessness and impermanence, which can lead to liberation from suffering. The second turning expanded on the first, the fruition of its teachings on the emptiness of all phenomena and universal compassion is Buddhahood. The teachings of the third turning are those on the buddha potential and its inherent qualities. For a detailed account of the three wheels of dharma see Thrangu Rinpoche's *The Three Vehicles of Buddhist Practice* published by Namo Buddha Publications.
53. Garma Chang. *The Hundred Thousand Songs of Milarepa,* pages 421-441.
54. Tib. *sil ba'i tshal* which means "The Cool Grove." It is described as

being just outside Rajghir, the then capital of Maghada, but various other locations are given, such as south-east of Bodhgaya.

55. Tilopa was the first to obtain the formless dakini teachings. Having traveled to Uddiyana, he received them directly from the formless wisdom dakini in a spiritual song. Basically, this song was comprised of nine instructions: 1. Loosen the seal knot of mind as ripening and freeing, 2. Look at the mirror of mind as samaya, 3. Slash water with a sword as activity, 4. Sun yourself in realization as samaya substance, 5. Look at the torch of wisdom as insight, 6. Turn the wheel of the web of nadi and prana, 7. Look at the outer mirror as equal taste, 8. Meditate on self-liberated Mahamudra, 9. Hold the jewel of the great bliss teachings.

56. Garma Chang. *The Hundred Thousand Songs of Milarepa.* Pages 463-498.

57. Tib. *snying-rje pad-ma dkar-po or* the *White Lotus of Compassion Sutra.*

58. Though the Tibetan is literally blue, this color/word is used for animals and people to denote dark gray or dark skinned.

59. A particular kind of Tibetan spirit believed to particularly be interested in influencing religious practitioners for its own ends.

60. Tib. *mi-gyo-ba.* The principal protector deity of the early Kadampas.

61. Gampopa was at this time a monk and drinking alcohol would have broken his vows.

62. A word based on a red sediment believed to be the menstrual blood of dakinis at sacred places, or a red powder substitute.

63. The word "look" is used here, but clearly this has nothing to do with sight. The word is used to contrast it with analyzing or examining which has an analytical, cognitive component which isn't present in "looking" at mind. So looking at mind implies direct and non-conceptual examination.

64. This is the translation of the Tibetan word *salwa* which is also translated variously as "brilliance," "luminous clarity," and "luminosity." We must not make the mistake of thinking of this as

some kind of light such as we get from a light bulb even though the words suggest this. Rather it is simply that continuous awareness, that knowing, that the mind always has.

65. Garma Chang. *The Hundred Thousand Songs of Milarepa,* "The Evidence of Accomplishment." Pages 658-661.

66. Tib. *brag dmar* meaning "Red-Rock." This mountain is the location of the chapter's events.

67. The obscuration of defilements prevents liberation and the obscuration of knowledge prevents omniscience.

68. The eight worldly dharmas are a concern with gain and loss, happiness and suffering, praise and criticism, fame and obscurity.

69. The ultimate or supreme siddhi is the stable realization of the radiant clarity or clear light nature of mind and all reality, which we know as complete and perfect enlightenment or Buddhahood. The relative siddhis are such qualities as loving kindness, compassion, intelligence, the wisdom of insight, spiritual power, protection, the removal of obstacles, good health, longevity, wealth and magnetism etc. – *Khenchen Thrangu Rinpoche*

Glossary of Terms

84,000 teachings. (Tib. *cho kyi phung po gyad khri bzhi stong*) 21,000 teachings on each of the Vinaya, Sutra, Abhidharma, and their combination. Their purpose is to eliminate the 84,000 different types of disturbing emotions latent in one's mind.

Abhidharma. (Tib. *chö ngön pa*) The Buddhist teachings are often divided into the Tripitaka: the sutras (teachings of the Buddha), the Vinaya (teachings on conduct,) and the Abhidharma which are the analyses of phenomena that exist primarily as a commentarial tradition to the Buddhist teachings.

Afflicted consciousness. (Tib. *nyön yid*) The seventh consciousness. As used here it has two aspects: the immediate consciousness which monitors the other consciousnesses making them continuous and the klesha consciousness which is the continuous presence of self. (see *consciousnesses, eight*)

Aggregates, five. (Skt. *skandha*, Tib. *phung po nga*) Literally, "heaps." These are the five basic transformations that perceptions undergo when an object is perceived. First is form, which includes all sounds, smells, etc., everything that is not thought. The second and third are sensations (pleasant and unpleasant, etc.) and their identification. Fourth are mental events, which actually include the second and third aggregates. The fifth is ordinary consciousness, such as the sensory and mental consciousnesses.

Amitayus. Skt. (Tib. *Tse pag me*) The name means infinitive life., Buddha of long life. Amitayus is the sambhogakaya form of Amitabhand a usually depicted with all the ornaments of a sambhogakaya Buddha.

Atisha. (982-1055 C.E.) A Buddhist scholar at the Nalanda University in India who came to Tibet at the invitation of the King to overcome the damage done by Langdarma. He helped found the Kadampa tradition.

Blessings. (Tib. *chin lap)* Splendour wave, conveying the sense of atmosphere descending or coming toward the practitioner. One's root guru and lineage are said to be the source of blessings. When the student can open themselves with uncontrived devotion, the grace of the lineage manifests as blessings, which dissolve into them and awaken them to a sense of greater reality.

Bodhichitta. (Tib. *chang chup chi sem)* Literally, the mind of enlightenment. There are two kinds of bodhichitta: absolute bodhichitta, which is completely awakened mind that sees the emptiness of phenomena, and relative bodhichitta which is the aspiration to practice the six paramitas and free all beings from the suffering of samsara. In regard to relative bodhichitta there is also two kinds: aspiration bodhichitta and perseverance bodhichitta.

Bodhisattva. (Tib. *chang chup sem pa*.) "Heroic mind." *Bodhi* means blossomed or enlightened, and *sattva* means heroic mind. Literally, one who exhibits the mind of enlightenment. Also an individual who has committed him or herself to the Mahayana path of compassion and the practice of the six paramitas to achieve Buddhahood to free all beings from samsara. These are the heart or mind disciples of the Buddha.

Bodhisattva levels. (Skt. *bhumi,* Tib. *sa*) The levels or stages a bodhisattva goes through to reach enlightenment. These consist of ten levels in the sutra tradition and thirteen in the tantra tradition.

Buddha. (Tib. *sang gye*) An individual who attains, or the attainment of, complete enlightenment, such as the historical Shakyamuni Buddha.

Buddha Shakyamuni. (Tib. *shakya tubpa*) The Shakyamuni Buddha, often called the Gautama Buddha, refers to the fourth Buddha of this age, who lived between 563 and 483 BCE.

Buddhafield. (Tib. *sang gye kyi zhing*) 1) One of the realms of the five Buddha families, either as sambhogakaya or nirmanakaya. 2) Pure personal experience.

Buddhahood. (Tib. *sang gyas*) The perfect and complete enlightenment of dwelling in neither samsara nor nirvana. Expression of the realization of perfect enlightenment, which characterizes a Buddha. The attainment of Buddhahood is the birthright of all beings. According to the teachings of Buddha, every sentient being has, or better is already, buddha nature; thus Buddhahood cannot be "attained." It is much more a matter of experiencing the primordial perfection and realizing it in everyday life.

Buddha nature. (Tib. *de shegs nying po*) The essential nature of all sentient beings. The potential for enlightenment.

Chakravartin. (Tib. *koro gyur wa*) Literally, the turner of the wheel and also called a universal monarch. This is a king who propagates the dharma and starts a new era.

Chakrasamvara. (Tib. *korlo dompa*) A meditational deity which belongs to the Anuttarayoga tantra set of teachings. A main yidam or tantra of the New Schools.

Chöd. (Tib.) This is pronounced "chö" and literally means "to cut off" and refers to a practice that is designed to cut off all ego involvement and defilements. The *mo chöd* (female chöd) practice was founded by the famous female saint Machig Labdron (1031 to 1129 C. E.).

Clarity. (Tib. *salwa*) Also translated as luminosity. The nature of mind is that it is empty of inherent existence, but the mind is not just voidness or completely empty because it has this clarity which is awareness or the knowing of mind. So clarity is a characteristic of emptiness (*shunyata*) of mind.

Completion stage. (Tib. *dzo rim*) In the Vajrayana there are two stages of meditation: the creation/development stage and the completion stage. Completion stage with marks is the six doctrines. Completion stage without marks is the practice of essence Mahamudra, resting in the unfabricated nature of mind.

Conventional level. There are two levels or truths: relative truth and ultimate truth. Relative truth describes the superficial and apparent mode of all things. Ultimate truth describes the true and unmistaken mode of all things. These two are described differently in the different schools, each progressively deeper leading closer to the way things are.

Creation stage. (Skt. *utpattikrama*, Tib. *che rim*) In the Vajrayana there are two stages of meditation: the development and the completion stage. The creation stage is a method of tantric meditation that involves the visualization and contemplation of deities for the purpose of purifying habitual tendencies and realizing the purity of all phenomena. In this stage visualization of the deity is established and maintained.

Daka. (Tib. *khandro*) A male counterpart to a dakini.

Dakini. (Tib. *khandroma*) A yogini who has attained high realizations of the fully enlightened mind. She may be a human being who has achieved such attainments or a non-human manifestation of the enlightened mind of a meditational deity. A female aspect of the protectors. It is feminine energy which has inner, outer and secret meanings.

Definitive meaning. The Buddha's teachings that state the direct meaning of dharma. They are not changed or simplified for the capacity of the listener, in contrast to the provisional meaning.

Dharani. A particular type of mantra, usually quite long.

Dharma. (Tib. *chö*) This has two main meanings: first, any truth, such as that the sky is blue; and secondly, the teachings of the Buddha (also called "Buddha-dharma").

Dharma protector. (Skt. *dharmapala*, Tib. *cho kyong*) A Buddha, bodhisattva or powerful but ordinary being whose job is to remove all interferences and bestow all necessary conditions for the practice of pure dharma.

Dharmadhatu. (Tib. *chö ying*) The all-encompassing space, unoriginated and without beginning, out of which all phenomena arises. The Sanskrit means "the essence of phenomena" and the Tibetan means "the expanse of phenomena," but it usually refers to the emptiness that is the essence of phenomena.

Dharmakaya. (Tib. *chö ku*) One of the three bodies of Buddhahood. It is enlightenment itself, that is, wisdom beyond any point of reference. (see *kayas, three.*)

Dharmata. (Tib. *chö nyi*) Dharmata is often translated as "suchness" or "the true nature of things" or "things as they are." It is phenomena as it really is or as seen by a completely enlightened being without any distortion or obscuration, so one can say it is "reality." The nature of phenomena and mind.

Disturbing emotions. (Skt. *klesha*, Tib. *nyön mong*) Also called the "afflictive emotions," these are the emotional afflictions or obscurations (in contrast to intellectual obscurations) that disturb the clarity of perception. These are also translated as "poisons." They include any emotion that disturbs or distorts consciousness. The main kleshas are desire, anger and ignorance.

Dzogchen. (Skt. *mahasandhi*) Literally "the great perfection" The teachings beyond the vehicles of causation, first taught in the human world by the great vidyadhara Garab Dorje.

Eight consciousnesses. The all-ground consciousness, mind-consciousness, afflicted consciousness, and the five sense-consciousnesses. The Hinayana sutras generally discuss mind in terms of six consciousnesses, namely, the five sensory consciousnesses and the sixth mental consciousness. The Mahayana Cittamatra school (Mind-only) school talks about the eight consciousness in which the first six are the same but has the seventh and eighth consciousnesses added. In the Hinayana tradition the functions of the seventh and eighth consciousness are subsumed in the sixth mental consciousness.

Eight worldly concerns. (Tib. *jik ten chö gysh*) These keep one from the path; they are attachment to gain, attachment to pleasure, attachment to praise, attachment to fame, aversion to loss, aversion to pain, aversion to blame and aversion to a bad reputation.

Emptiness. (Skt. *shunyata*, Tib. *tong pa nyi*) Also translated as voidness. The Buddha taught in the second turning of the wheel of dharma that external phenomena and the internal phenomena or concept of self or "I" have no real existence and therefore are "empty."

Empowerment. (Tib. *wang*, Skt. *abhiseka*) The conferring of power or authorization to practice the Vajrayana teachings, the indispensable entrance door to tantric practice. To do a Vajrayana practice one must receive the empowerment from a qualified lama. One should also receive the practice instruction (Tib. *tri*) and the textual reading (Tib. *lung*).

Enlightenment. (Tib. *jang chub*) The definition varies according to the Buddhist tradition, usually the same as Buddhahood. The Hinayana tradition defines liberation as the freedom from rebirth in samsara, with mind free of ignorance and emotional conflict. The Mahayana tradition holds that enlightenment is not complete without development of compassion and commitment to use skilful means to liberate all sentient beings. In the Vajrayana teachings, the foregoing stages of enlightenment are necessary, but ultimate enlightenment is a thorough purification of ego and concepts. The final fruition of complete liberation transcends all duality and conceptualization.

Essential drops. (Tib. *tigle*, Skt *bindu*) Vital essence drops or spheres of psychic energy that are often visualized in Vajrayana practices.

Eternalism. (Tib. *rtag lta*) The belief that there is a permanent and causeless creator of everything; in particular, that one's identity or consciousness has a concrete essence which is independent, everlasting and singular.

Experience and realization. (Tib. *nyam togs*) An expression used for insight and progress on the path. "Experience" refers to temporary meditation experiences and "realization" to unchanging understanding of the nature of things.

Five Buddha families. (Tib. *rig nga*) These are the Buddha, Vajra, Ratna, Padma and Karma families.

Five dhyani Buddhas. Vairochana, Akshobhya, Ratnasambhava, Amitabha and Amoghasiddhi. They are the pure aspects of the five elements and five emotions.

Five degeneration's. 1) of the times, meaning the outer events of the world such as wars and social unrest are becoming worse, 2) of beings, meaning their mind-streams are becoming coarser, 3) length of life is becoming shorter, 4) increase in the emotional afflictions of beings, causing instability in their minds, 5) and degeneration of view, meaning people's understanding of reality is growing further from the truth. Based on these five degenerations we are now living in a dark age.

Five paths. (Tib. *lam nga*) According to the sutras there are five paths; the path of accumulation, the path of integration/junction, the path of seeing/insight, (attainment of the first bodhisattva level), the path of meditation, and the path of no more learning (Buddhahood). The five paths cover the entire process from beginning dharma practice to complete enlightenment.

Five defilements. (Tib. *ldug nga*) Temporary mental states that inhibit understanding: ignorance, pride, anger, desire, and jealousy. The three root poisons are ignorance, desire and anger.

Five wisdoms. The dharmadhatu wisdom, mirror-like wisdom, wisdom of equality, discriminating wisdom and all-accomplishing wisdom. They should not be understood as separate entities but rather as different functions of one's enlightened essence.

Four empowerments. (Tib. *wang shi*) The empowerments of vase, secret, wisdom-knowledge and precious word.

Four extremes. (Tib. *tha shi*) Existence, non-existence, both and neither.

Four ways of changing the mind. The four foundations of meditation. (Tib. *tun mong gi ngon dro shi*) These are the four thoughts that turn the mind toward dharma. They are reflection on precious human birth, impermanence and the inevitability of death, karma and its effects, and the pervasiveness of suffering in samsara.

Four immeasurables. Love, compassion, emphatic joy, and impartiality.

Four seals. The four main principles of Buddhism: all compounded phenomena are impermanent, everything defiled (with ego-clinging) is suffering, all phenomena are empty and devoid of a self-entity, and nirvana is perfect peace.

Four truths. The Buddha's first teachings. 1) All conditioned life is suffering. 2) All suffering is caused by ignorance. 3) Suffering can cease. 4) The eight-fold path leads to the end of suffering: right understanding, thought, speech, action, livelihood, effort, mindfulness and meditation.

Four Yogas of Mahamudra. (Tib. *phyag chen gyi nal byor zhi*) Four stages in Mahamudra practice: one-pointedness, simplicity, one taste and non-meditation.

Gampopa. (1079-1153 C.E.) One of the main lineage holders of the Kagyu lineage in Tibet. A student of Milarepa, he established the first Kagyu monastic monastery and is known also for writing the *Jewel Ornament of Liberation.*

Ganacakra. (Tib. *tog kyi kor lo*) This is a ritual feast offering which is part of a spiritual practice.

Gods. See six realms.

Ground consciousness. (Tib. *kün shi nam she*) According to the Cittamatra school this is the eighth consciousness and is often called the alaya consciousness or store-house consciousness. (See *eight consciousnesses*)

Guru. (Tib. *lama*) A teacher in the Tibetan tradition who has reached realization.

Guru yoga. (Tib. *lamay naljor*) A practice of devotion to the guru culminating in receiving his blessing and blending indivisibly with his mind. Also refers to the fourth practice of the preliminary practices of ngöndro.

Guhyasamaja tantra. (Tib. *sang pa dus pa*) Literally, "Assembly of Secrets." One of the major tantras and yidams of the New School. This is the "father tantra" of the Anuttarayoga, which is the highest of the four tantras. Guhyasamaja is the central deity of the vajra family.

Hevajra. (Tib. *kye dorje*) This is the "mother tantra" of the Anuttarayoga tantra, which is the highest of the four yogas. "He" is said to be an exclamation of joy. Hevajra transforms sense pleasures into joy through the realization of the identity of form and emptiness. He is depicted in two, four, six, twelve, and sixteen-armed forms, dancing in union with his consort, usually Nairatmya.

Hevajra tantra. (Tib. *kye dorje*) This is the "mother tantra" of the Anuttarayoga tantra, which is the highest of the four yogas.

Hinayana. (Tib. *tek pa chung wa*) Literally, the "lesser vehicle." The first of the three *yanas*, or vehicles. The term refers to the first teachings of the Buddha, which emphasized the careful examination of mind and its confusion. It is the foundation of Buddha's teachings focusing mainly on the four truths and the twelve interdependent links. The fruit is liberation for oneself.

Hungry ghosts. (Tib. *yid dvags*) One of the six classes of sentient beings. Such beings are tormented by their own impure karmic perception causing them to suffer tremendously from craving, hunger and thirst. It is said that even if they came upon a lake of pure fresh water, due to their heavy karmic obscurations, they would see it as an undrinkable pool of pus. Pretas are depicted with very large bodies and very thin necks.

Illusory body. (Tib. *gyu lu*) The transformation of a practitioner's very subtle energy body into a deathless miracle body of the deity during the completion stages. When this is purified it becomes the form body of the Buddha, one of the Six Yogas of Naropa. (see *Six Yogas of Naropa*)

Jealous gods. See six realms.

Kadampa. (Tib.) One of the major schools in Tibet, it was founded by Atisha (993-1054 C.E.).

Kanjur. The preserved collection of the direct teaching of the Buddha.

Kagyu. (Tib.) *Ka* means oral and *gyu* means lineage; The lineage of oral transmission. One of the four major schools of Buddhism in Tibet. It was founded in Tibet by Marpa and is headed by His Holiness Karmapa. The other three are the Nyingma, the Sakya and the Gelugpa schools.

Karma. (Tib. *lay*) Literally "action." The unerring law of cause and effect, e.g., positive actions bring happiness and negative actions bring suffering. The actions of each sentient being are the causes that create the conditions for rebirth and the circumstances in that lifetime.

Karma Kagyu. (Tib.) One of the eight schools of the Kagyu lineage of Tibetan Buddhism which is headed by His Holiness Karmapa.

Karmapa. The name means Buddha activities. The Karmapas are the head of the Kagyu school of Buddhism and were the first to implement the tradition of incarnate lamas. Karmapas are thought to be an emanation of the bodhisattva Avalokiteshvara.

Key instructions — a text's key instruction rests upon establishing the line of reasoning in a teaching. Seeing this line of reasoning, we can distinguish between the form and the content of the teachings. What key instructions do are wake a person up to the true nature of the experience that the teachings generate, such as the dissolving of the objective form of the experience, which can be seen as it truly is, appreciated as having no independent reality and hence no power, as would be the case if it existed independently. The key instruction that, if acted upon, generates a liberating personality transformation, is repeated at each level of the teachings.

Klesha. (Tib. *nyön mong*) Also called the "disturbing emotions," these are the emotional afflictions or obscurations (in contrast to intellectual obscurations) that disturb the clarity of perception. These are also translated as "poisons." They include any emotion that disturbs or distorts consciousness. The three main kleshas are desire, anger and ignorance. The five kleshas are the three above plus pride and envy/jealousy.

Lama. (Skt. *guru*) *La* nobody above himself or herself in spiritual experience and *ma* expressing compassion like a mother. Thus the union of wisdom and compassion, feminine and masculine qualities. Lama is also a title given to a practitioner who has completed some extended training.

Latencies. (Skt. *vasana*. Tib. *bakchak*) Patterns of conditional response that exist as traces or tendencies stored in the alaya-vijnana, the eighth consciousness sometimes called the store-house or all-base consciousness. So called because it is a repository of all karmically conditioned patterns. All dualistic or ego-oriented experiences leave a residue, which is stored in the alaya-vijnana until a later time when some conscious occurrence activates the habitual pattern. The pattern then generates a response in the form of a perception or an action. This response leaves its own karmic residue, stored again in the unconscious repository, and the cycle continues. The explanation of this system is a central teaching of the Cittamatrin tradition of Mahayana Buddhism.

Liberation. (see *enlightenment*)

Lotsawa. Sanskrit for "translator."

Luminosity. (Tib. *salwa*) In the third turning of the wheel of dharma, the Buddha taught that everything is void, but this voidness is not completely empty because it has luminosity. Luminosity or clarity allows all phenomena to appear and is a characteristic of and inseparable from emptiness (Skt. *shunyata*).

Luminosity. (Tib. *osel*) Literally "free from the darkness of unknowing and endowed with the ability to cognize." The two aspects are "empty luminosity," like a clear open sky; and "manifest luminosity," such as colored light images, and so forth. Luminosity is the uncompounded nature present throughout all of samsara and nirvana.

Mahamudra. (Tib. *cha ja chen po*) Literally means "great seal" or "great symbol" meaning that all phenomena are sealed by the primordially perfect true nature. This form of meditation is traced back to Saraha (10th century) and was passed down in the Kagyu school through Marpa. This meditative transmission emphasizes perceiving mind directly rather than through rational analysis. It also refers to the experience of the practitioner where one attains the union of emptiness and luminosity and also perceives the non-duality of the phenomenal world and emptiness; also the name of Kagyupa lineage.

Mahapandita. (Tib. *pan di ta chen po*) *Maha* means great and *pandita* Buddhist scholar.

Mahasiddha. (Tib. *drup thop chen po)* A practitioner who has a great deal of realization. *Maha* means great and *siddha* refers to an accomplished practitioner. These were particularly Vajrayana practitioners who lived in India between the eight and twelfth century and practiced tantra. The biography of some of the most famous is found in *The Eighty-four Mahasiddhas.*

Mahayana. (Tib. *tek pa chen po*) Literally, the "Great Vehicle." These are the teachings of the second turning of the wheel of dharma, which emphasize shunyata (see *shunyata*), compassion and universal buddha nature. The purpose of enlightenment is to liberate all sentient beings from suffering as well as oneself. Mahayana schools of philosophy appeared several hundred years after the Buddha's death, although the tradition is traced to a teaching he is said to have given at Rajgriha, or Vulture Peak Mountain.

Maitripa - was a guru of Marpa, the Tibetan forefather of the Kagyu lineage. Thus it is through Maitripa that Maitreya and Asanga's crucial work on Buddha nature, the Uttaratantrasastra (*Anuttara*), became widely followed in Tibet. It is said that he had been a student of Naropa when the latter was head of Nalanda monastic university. Maitripa also transmitted to Marpa the esoteric aspect of Buddha nature embodied in the Mahamudra teachings, which treat the topic of mind in great detail and provide a wide range of progressive, highly refined meditations. Maitripa was brought to enlightenment through Mahamudra under his guru Savari, who received the complete teachings of Mahamudra from Nagarjuna, who received them from Sahara, whom Marpa encountered in his dream state.

Maitreya. The Loving One. The bodhisattva regent of Buddha Shakyamuni, presently residing in the Tushita heaven until becoming the fifth Buddha of this kalpa.

Mandala. (Tib. *chil kor*) Literally "centre and surrounding" but has different contexts. A diagram used in various Vajrayana practices that usually has a central deity and four directions.

Mantra. (Tib. *ngags*) 1) A synonym for Vajrayana. 2) A particular combination of sounds symbolizing the nature of a deity, for example OM MANI PEME HUNG (Tib. *ngak*). These are invocations to various meditation deities which are recited in Sanskrit. These Sanskrit syllables, representing various energies, are repeated in different Vajrayana practices.

Mantrayana. Another term for the Vajrayana.

Mara. (Tib. *du*) Difficulties encountered by the practitioner. The Tibetan word means heavy or thick. In Buddhism mara symbolizes the passions that overwhelm human beings as well as everything that hinders the arising of wholesome roots and progress on the path to enlightenment. There are four kinds: *skandha-mara*, which is incorrect view of self; *klesha-mara*, which is being overpowered by negative emotions; *matyu-mara*, which is death and interrupts spiritual practice; and *devaputra-mara*, which is becoming stuck in the bliss that comes from meditation.

Marpa. (1012-1097 C.E.) Marpa was known for being a Tibetan who made three trips to India and brought back many tantric texts, including the Six Yogas of Naropa, the Guhyasamaja, and the Chakrasamvara practices. His root teacher was Tilopa, the founder of the Kagyu lineage and the teacher of Naropa. Marpa initiated and founded the Kagyu lineage in Tibet.

Mental consciousness. (Tib. *yid kyi namshe*) The sixth consciousness is the faculty of thinking which produces thoughts based upon the experiences of the five sense consciousnesses or its own previous content. (see *eight consciousnesses*).

Mental factors. (Tib. *sem yung*) Mental factors are contrasted to mind in that they are more long-term propensities of mind including eleven virtuous factors such as faith, detachment, and equanimity, and the six root defilements such as desire, anger, and pride, and the twenty secondary defilements such as resentment, dishonesty, harmfulness.

Milarepa. (1040-1123 C.E.) Milarepa was a student of Marpa who attained enlightenment in one lifetime. *Mila,* named by the deities and *repa* means white cotton. His student Gampopa established the (*Dagpo*) Kagyu lineage in Tibet.

Mind-only school. Also called Cittamatra school. This is one of the major schools in the Mahayana tradition founded in the fourth century by Asanga that emphasized everything is mental events.

Mudra. (Tib. *chak gya*) In this book it is a "hand seal" or gesture that is performed in specific tantric rituals to symbolize certain aspects of the practice being done. Also can mean spiritual consort, or the "bodily form" of a deity.

Nadi. The channels in the vajra body through which the winds flow.

Naropa. (956-1040 C.E.) An Indian master best known for transmitting many Vajrayana teachings to Marpa who took these back to Tibet before the Moslem invasion of India.

Nihilism. (Tib. *chad lta*) Literally, "the view of discontinuance." The extreme view of nothingness: no rebirth or karmic effects, and the non-existence of a mind after death.

Nirmanakaya. (Tib. *tulku*) There are three bodies of the Buddha and the nirmanakaya or "emanation body" manifests in the world and in this context manifests as the Shakyamuni Buddha. (see *kayas, three.*)

Nirvana. (Tib. *nyangde*) Literally, "extinguished." Individuals live in samsara and with spiritual practice can attain a state of enlightenment in which all false ideas and conflicting emotions have been extinguished. This is called nirvana. The nirvana of a Hinayana practitioner is freedom from cyclic existence, an arhat. The nirvana of a Mahayana practitioner is Buddhahood, free from extremes of dwelling in either samsara or the perfect peace of an arhat.

Nondistraction. (Tib. *yengs med*) Not straying from the continuity of the practice.

Nonfabrication. (Tib. *zo med*) The important key point in meditation of Mahamudra and Dzogchen; that inate wakefulness is not created through intellectual effort.

Nonmeditation. (Tib. *gom med*) The state of not holding on to an object meditated upon nor a subject who meditates. Also refers to the fourth stage of Mahamudra in which nothing further needs to be meditated upon or cultivated.

Nonthought. (Tib. *mi tog*) A state in which conceptual thinking is absent.

Obscurations. There are two categories of obscurations or defilements that cover one's buddha nature: the defilement of disturbing emotions (see *five poisons & afflictive obscurations*) and the defilement of latent tendencies or sometimes called the obscuration of dualistic perception, or the intellectual/cognitive obscurations. The first category prevents sentient beings from freeing themselves from samsara, while the second prevents them from gaining accurate knowledge and realising truth.

Occurrence. (Tib. *gyu ba*) The period when thoughts are arising in the mind. Compare with "stillness."

One-pointedness. (Tib. *Tse cig*) The first stage in the practice of Mahamudra.

One taste, (Tib. *ro cig*) The third stage in the practice of Mahamudra.

Oral transmission. As opposed to the scholastic traditions, the oral instructions of the Practice lineages are concise and pithy so they can always be kept in mind; they are practical and to the point so they are effective means to deal directly with the practice.

Pandita. A great scholar.

Paramita. "Transcendental" or "Perfection." Pure actions free from dualistic concepts that liberate sentient beings from samsara. The six paramitas are: generosity, diligence, patience, morality, contemplation, and transcendental knowledge or insight.

Path of Liberation. (Tib. *drol lam*) The path of Mahamudra practice.

Path of Means. (Tib. *thab lam*) Refers to the Six Yogas of Naropa as well as to the stages of creation and completion with attributes.

Phowa. (Tib.) There are different kinds of phowa practice. The highest result of *dharmakaya phowa* and *sambhogakaya phowa* is full enlightenment. In this text, reference has primarily been to *nirmanakaya phowa*, called "the phowa that one practices" and *Kacho Phowa*, an advanced tantric practice of dream yoga and clear light yoga concerned with the ejection of consciousness at death to a favourable realm or rebirth.

Pointing-out instructions. (Tib. *ngo sprod kyi gdampa*) The direct introduction to the nature of mind.

Prana. Life supporting energy. The "winds" or energy-currents of the vajra body.

Prajnaparamita. (Tib. *she rab chi parol tu chinpa)* Transcendent perfect knowledge. The Tibetan literally means, "gone to the other side" or "gone beyond" as expressed in the prajnaparamita mantra, "Om gate gate paragate parasamgate bodhi svaha." The realization of emptiness in the Prajnaparamita Hridaya or Heart Sutra made possible by the extraordinarily profound dharma of the birth of Shakyamuni Buddha in the world and the practices that came from it, such as the Vajrayana tantras, which make use of visualization and the control of subtle physical energies.

Prajnaparamita sutras. Used to refer to a collection of about 40 Mahayana sutras that all deal with the realization of prajna.

Pratyekabuddha. "Solitary Awakened One." These are the body disciples of the Buddha. One who has attained awakening for himself, and on his own, with no teacher in that life. Generally placed on a level between arhat and Buddha. It is the fruition of the second level of the Hinayana path through contemplation on the twelve interdependent links in reverse order.

Provisional meaning. The teachings of the Buddha which have been simplified or modified to the capabilities of the audience. This contrasts with the definitive meaning.

Recognition. (Tib. *ngo shes, ngo phrod*) In this context it means "recognizing the nature of mind."

Relative truth. (Tib. *kunsop*) There are two truths: relative and absolute or ultimate truth. Relative truth is the perception of an ordinary (unenlightened) being who sees the world with all his or her projections based on the false belief in "I" and "other."

Root guru. (Tib. *tsa way lama*) A practitioner of Vajrayana can have several types of root guru: the vajra master who confers empowerment, who bestows reading transmission, or who explains the meaning of the tantras. The ultimate root guru is the master who gives the "pointing out instructions" so that one recognizes the nature of mind.

Sacred outlook. (Tib. *dag snang*) Awareness and compassion lead the practitioner to experience emptiness (*shunyata*). From that comes luminosity manifesting as the purity and sacredness of the phenomenal world. Since the sacredness comes out of the experience of emptiness, the absence of preconceptions, it is neither a religious nor a secular vision: that is, spiritual and secular vision could meet. Moreover, sacred outlook is not conferred by any god. Seen clearly, the world is self-existingly sacred.

Sakya Pandita. A hereditary head of the Sakya lineage. A great scholar (1181-1251 C.E.)

Samadhi. (Tib. *tin ne zin*) A state of meditation that is non-dualistic. There is an absence of discrimination between self and other. Also called meditative absorption or one-pointed meditation; this is the highest form of meditation.

Samantabhadra. *Samanta* means all and *bhadra* means excellent. "He who is All-pervadingly Good" or "He whose Beneficence is Everywhere." There are two Samantabhadras, one is the dharmakaya and the other is one of the eight main bodhisattvas, embodiment of all Buddhas aspirations. In the Vajrayana tradition Samantabhadra is the primordial Buddha and representative of the experiential content of the dharmakaya.

Samaya. (Tib. *dam sig*) The vows or commitments made in the Vajrayana to a teacher or to a practice. Many details exist but essentially it consists of outwardly, maintaining a harmonious relationship with the vajra master and one's dharma friends and inwardly, not straying from the continuity of the practice.

Sambhogakaya. (Tib. *long chö dzok ku*) There are three bodies of the Buddha and the sambhogakaya, also called the "enjoyment body," is a realm of the dharmakaya that only manifests to bodhisattvas (see *kayas, three*).

Samsara. (Tib. *kor wa*) "Cyclic existence." The conditioned existence of ordinary life in which suffering occurs because one still possesses attachment, aggression and ignorance. It is contrasted to nirvana. Through the force of karma motivated by ignorance, desire and anger one is forced to take on the impure aggregates and circle the wheel of existence until liberation.

Sangha. (Tib. *gen dun*) "Virtuous One." *Sang* means intention or motivation and *gha* means virtuous. One with virtuous motivation. One of the three jewels. Generally refers to the followers of Buddhism, and more specifically to the community of monks and nuns. The exalted sangha is those who have attained a certain level of realization of the Buddha's teachings.

Secret mantra. (Tib. *sang ngak*) A name for the Vajrayana.

Selflessness. (Tib. *dag me*) Also called egolessness. In two of the Hinayana schools (Vaibhashika and Sautrantika) this referred exclusively to the fact that "a person" is not a real permanent self, but rather just a collection of thoughts and feelings. In two of the Mahayana schools (Cittamatra and Madhyamaka) this was extended to mean there was no inherent existence to outside phenomena as well.

Sending and taking practice. (Tib. *tong len*) A meditation practice promulgated by Atisha in which the practitioner takes on the negative conditions of others and gives out all that is positive.

Sentient beings. With consciousness, an animated being as opposed to an inanimate object. All beings with consciousness or mind who have not attained the liberation of Buddhahood. This includes those individuals caught in the sufferings of samsara as well as those who have attained the levels of a bodhisattva.

Shamatha. (Tib.) See tranquillity meditation.

Shamatha with support. (Tib. *shinay ten cas*) The practice of calming the mind while using an object of concentration, material or mental, or simply the breath.

Shamatha without support. (Tib. *shinay ten med*) The act of calming the mind without any particular object, resting undistractedly. This practice serves as a prelude for Mahamudra and should not be mistaken for the ultimate result.

Shunyata. See emptiness.

Siddha. (Tib. *drup top)* An accomplished Buddhist practitioner.

Siddhi. (Tib. *ngodrup*) "Accomplishment." The spiritual accomplishments of accomplished practitioners. Usually refers to the "supreme siddhi" of complete enlightenment, but can also mean the "common siddhis," eight mundane accomplishments.

Simplicity. (Tib. *spros ral*) 1) The absence of creating mental constructs or conceptual formations about the nature of things. 2) The second stage in the practice of Mahamudra.

Six realms. (Tib. *rikdruk*) The realms of the six classes of beings: gods, demigods, humans, animals, hungry ghosts and hell beings. These are the possible types of rebirths for beings in samsara and are: the god realm in which gods have great pride, the jealous god realm in which the jealous gods try to maintain what they have, the human realm which is the best realm because one has the possibility of achieving enlightenment, the animal realm characterized by stupidity, the hungry ghost realm characterized by great craving, and the hell realm characterized by aggression.

Six Yogas of Naropa. (Tib. *naro chödruk*) These six special yogic practices were transmitted from Naropa to Marpa and consist of the subtle heat practice, the illusory body practice, the dream yoga practice, the luminosity practice, the ejection of consciousness practice and the bardo practice.

Skandha. (Tib. *pung pa*) Literally "heaps." These are the five basic transformations that perceptions undergo when an object is perceived: form, feeling, perception, formation and consciousness. First is form, which includes all sounds, smells, etc.; everything we usually think of as outside the mind. The second and third are sensations (pleasant and unpleasant, etc.) and their identification. Fourth is mental events, which include the second and third aggregates. The fifth is ordinary consciousness, such as the sensory and mental consciousnesses.

Skilful means. Ingenuity in application.

Spiritual song. (Skt. *doha*, Tib. *gur*) A religious song spontaneously composed by a Vajrayana practitioner. It usually has nine syllables per line.

Stillness. (Tib. *gnas pa*) Absence of thought activity and disturbing emotions, but with subtle fixation on this stillness.

Subtle winds, channels, and essences. Prana, nadi, and bindu; the constituents of the vajra body. These channels are not anatomical structures, but more like meridians in acupuncture. There are thousands of channels, but the three main channels that carry the subtle energy are the right, left and central channel. The central channel runs roughly along the spinal column while the right and left are on the sides of the central channel.

According to the yogic teachings of the path of skilful means, realization is attained through synchronization of body and mind. This may be achieved through meditating on nadi (channels), prana (energy), and bindu (drops) – the psychic components in the illusory body. Prana is the energy, or "wind," moving through the nadis. As is said, "Mind consciousness rides the horse of prana on the pathways of the nadis. The bindu is mind's nourishment."

Because of dualistic thinking, prana enters the left and right channels. This divergence of energy in the illusory body corresponds to the mental activity that falsely distinguishes between subject and object and leads to karmically determined activity. Through yogic practice, the pranas can be brought into the central channel and therefore transformed into wisdom-prana. Then the mind can recognize its fundamental nature, realizing all dharmas as unborn. This belongs to advanced practice and can only be learned through direct oral transmission from an accomplished guru. Once the meditator is well established in the experience of the fundamental nature of mind, they can meditate on it directly, dissolving the nadi, prana, and bindu visualization. Meditation using the concept of psychic channels is regarded as being the completion stage with signs, and the formless practice which contemplates the nature of mind directly is the completion stage without signs

Supreme siddhi. Another word for enlightenment.

Sutra. (Tib. *do*) Literally "Junction." The combination of the Hinayana and Mahayana, or the combination of wisdom and compassion. Texts in the Buddhist cannon attributed to the Buddha. They are viewed as his recorded words, although they were not actually written down until many years after his *paranirvana.* They are usually in the form of dialogues between the Buddha and his disciples. These are often contrasted with the tantras which are the Buddha's Vajrayana teachings and the shastras which are commentaries on the words of the Buddha.

Sutra Mahamudra. (Tib. *mdo'i phyag chen*) The Mahamudra system based on the Prajnaparamita scriptures and emphasizing Shamatha and Vipashyana and the progressive journey through the five paths and ten bhumis.

Sutrayana. The sutra approach to achieving enlightenment which includes the Hinayana and the Mahayana.

Svabhavakakaya. (Tib. *ngo bo nyid kyi sku*) The "essence body." Sometimes counted as the fourth kaya, the unity of the first three.

Tantra. (Tib. *gyu.*) Literally, tantra means "continuity," and in Buddhism it refers to two specific things: the texts (resultant texts, or those that take the result as the path) that describe the practices leading from ignorance to enlightenment, including commentaries by tantric masters; and the way to enlightenment itself, encompassing the ground, path, and fruition. One can divide Buddhism into the sutra tradition and the tantra tradition. The sutra tradition primarily involves the academic study of the Mahayana sutras and the tantric path primarily involves practicing the Vajrayana practices. The tantras are primarily the texts of the Vajrayana practices.

Tantra Mahamudra. (Tib. *sngags kyi phyag chen*) The same as mantra Mahamudra. The Mahamudra practice connected to the six dharmas of Naropa.

Tara. (Tib. *drol ma*) An emanation of Avalokiteshvara, she is said to have arisen from one of his tears. She embodies the female aspect of compassion and is a very popular deity in Tibet. Her two common iconographic forms are white and green.

Three jewels. (Tib. *kön chok sum*) Literally "three precious ones." The three essential components of Buddhism: Buddha, dharma, sangha, i.e., the Awakened One, the truth expounded by him, and the followers living in accordance with this truth. Firm faith in the three precious ones is the stage of "stream entry." The three precious ones are objects of veneration and are considered "places of refuge." The Buddhist takes refuge by pronouncing the threefold refuge formula, thus acknowledging formally to be a Buddhist.

Three kayas. Dharmakaya, sambhogakaya, and nirmanakaya. Fully enlightened beings, Buddhas, and their manifestations are often understood by way of the three kayas: The dharmakaya is enlightenment itself, wisdom beyond any reference point which can only be perceived by other enlightened beings; The sambhogakaya, often called the enjoyment body, manifests in the pure lands which can only be seen by advanced bodhisattvas; and the nirmanakaya which can be seen by ordinary beings as in the case of the historical Buddha, but this can also be any type of being or relative appearance to assist ordinary beings.

Three realms. These are three categories of samsara. The desire realm includes existences where beings are reborn with solid bodies due to their karma ranging from the deva paradises to the hell realms. The form realm is where beings are reborn due to the power of

meditation; and their bodies are of subtle form in this realm. These
are the meditation paradises. The formless realm is where beings
due to their meditation (samadhi), have entered a state of meditation
after death and the processes of thought and perception have ceased.

Three roots. Guru, yidam and dakini. Guru is the root of blessings,
yidam of accomplishment and dakini of activity.

Three sufferings. These are the suffering of suffering, the suffering of
change, and pervasive suffering (meaning the inherent suffering in
all of samsara).

Three vehicles. Hinayana, Mahayana and Vajrayana.

Tilopa. (928-1009 C.E.) One of the eighty-four mahasiddhas who
became the guru of Naropa who transmitted his teachings to the
Kagyu lineage in Tibet.

Tonglen. Giving and taking. A bodhichitta practice of giving one's virtue
and happiness to others and taking their suffering and misdeeds
upon oneself.

Torma. (Tib.) A sculpture made out of tsampa and moulded butter,
used as a shrine offering, a feast offering substance, or as a
representation of deities. There are traditional designs for each of
the many types of torma.

Tranquillity meditation. (Tib. *Shinay*, Skt. *Shamatha*) One of the two
main types of meditation, calm abiding, the meditative practice of
calming the mind in order to rest free from the disturbance of
thought activity, the other is insight.

Tsampa (Tib.) Dried barley flour that Tibetans eat by mixing with
butter.

Tummo. (Tib.) An advanced Vajrayana practice for combining bliss and
emptiness which produces heat as a by product. This is one of the
Six Yogas of Naropa.

Two accumulations. (Tib. *shogs nyis*) The accumulation of merit with
concepts and the accumulation of wisdom beyond concepts.

Ultimate truth. (Tib. *dondam*) There are two truths or views of reality:
relative truth which is seeing things as ordinary beings do with the

dualism of "I" and "other" and ultimate truth, which transcends duality and sees things as they are.

Vajra posture. This refers to the full-lotus posture in which the legs are interlocked. When one leg is placed before the other as many Westerners sit it is called the half-lotus posture.

Vajradhara. (Tib. *Dorje Chang*) "Holder of the vajra." *Vajra* means indestructible and *dhara* means holding, embracing or inseparable. The central figure in the Kagyu refuge tree, and indicating the transmission of the close lineage of the Mahamudra teachings to Tilopa. Vajradhara symbolizes the primordial wisdom of the dharmakaya and wears the ornaments of the sambhogakaya Buddha, symbolizing its richness.

Vajravarahi. (Tib. *Dorje Phagmo*) A dakini who is the consort of Chakrasamvara. She is the main yidam of the Kagyu lineage and the embodiment of wisdom.

Vajrayogini. (Tib. *Dorje Palmo*) A semi-wrathful yidam. Female.

Vajrayana. (Tib. *dorje tek pa*) Literally, "diamond-like" or "indestructible capacity." *Vajra* here refers to method, so you can say the method yana. There are three major traditions of Buddhism (Hinayana, Mahayana, Vajrayana) The Vajrayana is based on the tantras and emphasizes the clarity aspect of phenomena. A practitioner of the method of taking the result as the path.

View, meditation, and action. (Tib. *ta ba gom pa yodpa*) The philosophical orientation, the act of growing accustomed to that – usually in sitting practice, and the implementation of that insight during the activities of daily life. Each of the three vehicles has its particular definition of view, meditation and action.

Vipashyana meditation. (Tib. *lha tong*) Sanskrit for "insight meditation." This meditation develops insight into the nature of reality (Skt. *dharmata*). One of the two main aspects of meditation practice, the other being Shamatha.

Wheel of dharma. (Skt. *dharmachakra*) The Buddha's teachings correspond to three levels which very briefly are: the first turning was the teachings on the four noble truths and the teaching of the egolessness of person; the second turning was the teachings on emptiness and the emptiness of phenomena; the third turning was the teachings on luminosity and buddha nature.

Whispered lineage. Instructions that concern emptiness and that come from jnana yoga dakinis.

Yana. Means capacity. There are three yanas, narrow, (Hinayana) great (Mahayana) and indestructible (Vajrayana).

Yidam. (Tib.) *Yi* means mind and *dam* means pure, or *yi* means your mind and *dam* means inseparable. The yidam represents the practitioner's awakened nature or pure appearance. A tantric deity that embodies qualities of Buddhahood and is practiced in the Vajrayana. Also called a tutelary deity.

Yidam meditation. (Tib.) Yidam meditation is the Vajrayana practice that uses the visualization of a yidam.

Yoga. "Natural condition." A person who practices this is called a *yogi,* characterized by leaving everything natural, just as it is, e.g. not washing or cutting your hair and nails etc. A female practitioner is called a *yogini.*

Yogatantra. (Tib. *naljor gyi gyu*) Literally, "union tantra" and refers to a tantra that places emphasis on internal meditations.

Yogi. (Tib *nal yor pa*) Tantric practitioner.

Yogini. (Tib *nal yor ma*) Female tantric practitioner.

Glossary of Tibetan Terms

Pronounced	Spelled in Tibetan	English
bon	bon	Bon religion
ch ja chen po	phyag rgya chen po	Mahamudra
chang chup chi sem	byang chub sems dpa	bodhisattva
chin kor	dkyil 'khor	mandala
chod	gcod	cutting practice
chö	chos	dharma
chö ku	chos sku	dharmakaya
chö ngön pa	chos mngon pa	Abhidharma
damsig	dam tshig	samaya
do	mdo	sutra
Dorje Chang	rdo rje 'chang	Vajradhara
Dorje Phagmo	rdo rje phag mo	Vajravarahi
drup top	grub thob	siddha
gom	sgom	meditate
gur	mgur	spiritual song
Kadampa	bka' gdams pa	Kadampa
Kagyu	bka' brgyud	Kagyu
khandroma	mkha' 'gro ma	dakini
korlo gyur wa	'khor lo sdom pa	chakravartin
korwa	'khor ba	samsara
kön chok sum	dkon mchog gsum	three jewels
ku sum	sku gsum	kayas, three

Kungdu Sangmo	kun dga' bzong po	Samantabhadra
lama	bla ma	guru
lay	las	karma
lhag tong	lhag mthong	Vipashyana
lhen chik kye pay yeshe	lhan cig skyes pa'i ye shes	coemergent wisdom
nam tar	rnam thar	spiritual biography
naro chödruk	na ro chos drug	Six Yogas of Naropa
ngak	sngags	mantra
nyangde	myang 'das	nirvāna
nyen gyu	snyan rgyud	whispered trans.
nyön mong	nyon mongs	klesha
phowa	'pho ba	transfer of conscious.
phung po nga	pung po nga	five aggregates
rang sang gye	rang sangs rgyas	pratyekabuddha
repa	ras pa	tantric adept
sam ten	bsam gtan	dhyana meditation
sherab	shes rab	prajña
shine	zhi gnas	Shamatha
tan chö	bstan bcos	shastra
tek pa chen po	theg pa chan po	Mahayana
thab lam	thabs lam	skilful means
thö pa	thod pa	skull cup
tigle	thig le	subtle drop
tin ne zin	ting nge 'dzin	samadhi
tong len	glong len	giving and taking
tong pa nyi	strong pa nyid	emptiness
torma	gtor ma	ritual cakes
tummo	gtum mo	subtle heat
wang	dbang	empowerment
yeshe	ye shes	jñana

Bibliography

Mahamudra: The Ocean of Definitive Meaning.
Text by the Ninth Karmapa, Wangchuk Dorje. Nitartha Publications, 2001.

Pointing Out the Dharmakaya.
Text by the Ninth Karmapa, Wangchuk Dorje, commentary by Khenchen Thrangu Rinpoche. Auckland: Zhyisil Chokyi Ghatsal Publications, 2002.

The Hundred Thousand Songs of Milarepa.
Chang, Garma C.C. Boston and London: Shambhala Publications, 1999.

The Life of Marpa the Translator.
Nalanda Translation Committee. Boston and London: Shambhala, 1986.

The Life of Milarepa.
Lhalungpa, Lobsang P. Boston and London: Shambhala, 1985.

The Mahamudra Which Eliminates the Darkness of Ignorance.
Text by the Ninth Karmapa, Wangchuk Dorje, commentary Beru

Khyentse Rinpoche. New Delhi: Library of Tibetan Works and Archives, 1978.

The Rain of Wisdom.
Nalanda Translation Committee. Boston and London: Shambhala, 1999.

Index

Other publications from
Zhyisil Chokyi Ghatsal

A Guide to Shamatha Meditation
Buddhist Conduct: The Ten Virtuous Actions
The Life of the Buddha & The Four Noble Truths
The Twelve Links of Interdependent Origination
Teachings on the Practice of Meditation
Four Foundations of Buddhist Practice
The Three Vehicles of Buddhist Practice
The Middle Way Meditation Instructions
Ascertaining Certainty in the View
The Two Truths
Progressive Stages of Meditation on Emptiness
Beautiful Song of Marpa the Translator
Transcending Ego: Distinguishing Consciousness from Wisdom
An Introduction to Mahamudra Meditation
An Overview of the Bardo Teachings
The Five Buddha Families and the Eight Consciousnesses
The Four Dharmas of Gampopa
Aspirational Prayer for Mahamudra
Showing the Path of Liberation
Medicine Buddha Teachings
Journey of the Mind: teachings on the bardo
The Essence of Creation & Completion
Mahamudra Teachings
The Aspiration Prayer of Mahamudra
Pointing Out the Dharmakaya
The Life of Tilopa & The Ganges Mahamudra
A Spiritual Biography of Marpa the Translator
Rechungpa, A Biography of Milarepa's Disciple

Zhyisil Chokyi Ghatsal
PO Box 6259, Wellesley St, Auckland, New Zealand
Email: orders@greatliberation.org Website: www.greatliberation.org

149

Meditation Centre Information

For more information and instruction
please contact one of the following centres.

Rumtek Monastery
International Seat of His Holiness 17th Karmapa Urgyen Trinley Dorje
Sikkim, INDIA

Sherab Ling Buddhist Institute: Seat of His Eminence Tai Situpa
Kangra District, Himachal Pradesh, 176-125, INDIA
Ph: (01894) 63013/63757

New Zealand

Karma Choeling Buddhist Monastery
66 Bodhisattva Road
RD1 Kaukapakapa
Ph: 09 420 5428
www.kagyu.org.nz

Karma Thigsum Choeling
P.O. Box 3160
Christchurch
Ph: 03 384 4626

Kagyu Samten Choling
PO Box 917
Gisborne
Ph: 06 867 1956

Australia

Kagyu Thigsum Chokyi Ghatsal
PO Box 235, Newstead
Tasmania
Ph/fax: 03 6334 9680

Karma Tashi Choling
P.O. Box 973
Bega, NSW 2550
Ph: 02 6496 7169

Kagyu E-Vam Buddhist Institute
673 Lygon Street,
Carlton North, Vic. 3054
Ph: 03 9387 0422

For a list of Karma Kagyu Centres worldwide, contact:
Karma Triyana Dharmachakra
352 Meads Mt Rd, Woodstock, New York 12498
(914) 679-5906, email office@kagyu.org www.kagyu.org

Kagyu Samye Ling Monastery & Tibetan Centre
Eskdalemuir, Langholm, Dumfrieshire, Scotland, DG13 OQL
(013) 873 73232, email scotland@samyeling.org www.samyeling.org

Care of Dharma Books

Dharma books contain the teachings of the Buddha. They have the power to protect against lower rebirth and to point the way to Liberation. Therefore, they should be treated with respect, kept off the floor and places where people sit or walk, and not stepped over. They should be covered or protected for transporting and kept in a high, clean place separate from more "ordinary" things. If it is necessary to dispose of Dharma materials, they should be burned with care and awareness rather than thrown in the trash. When burning Dharma texts, it is considered skilful to first recite a prayer or mantra, such as OM, AH, HUNG. Then you can visualize the letters of the text (to be burned) being absorbed into the AH, and the AH being absorbed into you. After that you can burn the texts.

These considerations may be also kept in mind for Dharma artwork, as well as the written teachings and artwork of other religions.